DEPRIVATION
IN AMERICA

The Insight Series
Studies in Contemporary Issues
from Glencoe Press

PROBLEMS OF AMERICAN FOREIGN POLICY
Martin B. Hickman

THE OPPENHEIMER AFFAIR: a political play in three acts
Joseph Boskin and Fred Krinsky

THE POLITICS OF RELIGION IN AMERICA
Fred Krinsky

THE WELFARE STATE: who is my brother's keeper
Fred Krinsky and Joseph Boskin

OPPOSITION POLITICS: the anti — new deal tradition
Joseph Boskin

IS AMERICAN DEMOCRACY EXPORTABLE?
Edward G. McGrath

PROTEST FROM THE RIGHT
Robert A. Rosenstone

DEMOCRACY AND COMPLEXITY: who governs the governors?
Fred Krinsky

FERMENT IN LABOR
Jerome Wolf

AMERICAN ANTI-WAR MOVEMENTS
Joseph Conlin

THE POLITICS AND ANTI-POLITICS OF THE YOUNG
Michael Brown

URBAN RACIAL VIOLENCE IN THE TWENTIETH CENTURY
Joseph Boskin

POSTWAR AMERICA: the search for identity
Donald G. Baker and Charles H. Sheldon

BLACK POWER: the racial response to white America
Thomas Wagstaff

THE MEXICAN-AMERICANS: an awakening minority
Manuel P. Servin

THE SUPREME COURT: politicians in robes
Charles H. Sheldon

DEPRIVATION IN AMERICA: a case study in deprivation
Victor B. Ficker and Herbert S. Graves

BOYS NO MORE: some social-psychological aspects of the new block ethic
Charles W. Thomas

POLITICS OF THE NEW LEFT:
Matthew Stolz

THE MILITARY AND AMERICAN SOCIETY:
Martin B. Hickman

Series Editors: Fred Krinsky and Joseph Boskin

DEPRIVATION IN AMERICA

Victor B. Ficker
Chairman of the Social Sciences Department
Polk Junior College

and

Herbert S. Graves
Head of the Department of American Studies
Polk Junior College

GLENCOE PRESS
A Division of The Macmillan Company
Beverly Hills, California
Collier-Macmillan Ltd., London

To: Edith, Linda, Betty, Ellen, and Celene.
With affection and with the hope that your generation will witness an end to man's inhumanity to man.

CONTENTS

Preface

Deprivation is a word that has many varied meanings. We would all agree that deprivation in America is different from deprivation in India. Deprivation is relative.

This becomes a matter of small consolation, however, that, in America, nearly 30 million people live in conditions that wrong the dignity of man. Poverty figures are conveniently tossed about to illustrate whatever their users wish to prove. Yet the conditions presented in Michael Harrington's **The Other America** have changed little over the past decade. In many cases, the gap between the rich and the poor has widened. While our nation is hopefully beginning a swing to at least a moderate peace time economy, unemployment has become a serious problem.

A single book, a single government program, a single citizen cannot change the plight of the deprived. Only an enlightened, aroused citizenry can do anything to alter their awful conditions. **Deprivation in America** presents some of the most serious and debilitating factors in American life. Hopefully, awareness will lead to action. That remains in the hands and conscience of the reader.

V. B. F. and H. S. G.

WINTER HAVEN, FLORIDA
July, 1970

"NOTE — Throughout this book, the author–editor's footnotes are marked by symbols — *, † — and the original quoted notes by numerals.)"

Chapter One

You're Asking Me What Deprivation Is?

While deprivation is not a respecter of race, religion, or national origin, it does befall the lower social and economic groups of our society. It is often said that anyone with the desire to do so can climb out of his environment and forever be rid of the deprivations of poverty and want. See if you agree with that thought after you read the case study that follows.

This case study is not fiction—it is the *true* story of a woman of twenty-eight or twenty-nine years of age who looks more nearly fifty. The story is in the subject's own words—slightly cleaned up to eliminate the profanity and some of her bitter resentment toward a society which does not include her. It is her report to case worker in a field office of the Office of Economic Opportunity.

Read her story with compassion. It is one of desperation and utter hopelessness; it covers all categories of deprivation. This woman seems trapped in the bottom of a deep well with sides too steep to climb, with no handholes or ropes to grasp. If you feel no compassion for her, then think of her children, for she sees no way out for them either.

The authors have never read an account that better describes the many types of deprivation experienced by our disadvantaged citizens. Here in one package is what the present means for one family and what little hope exists for its future. The woman is white; the locale is Tennessee. She could just as easily have been Black, Mexican-American, or Puerto Rican—families such as hers exist in each of our fifty states. As a matter of fact, families such as this exist in all of our communities. We can find them if we only will look; we can help if only we take the trouble to understand and decide to help. Can we do less?

A Case Study In Deprivation*

Here I am, dirty, smelly, with no proper underwear beneath this rotting dress. I don't know about you, but the stench of my teeth makes me half sick. They're decaying, but they'll never be fixed. That takes money.

Listen to me without pity, now, for I don't need your pity; it won't help me at all, and it won't help my hungry children. Listen to me with understanding, if you can. Try to put yourself in my dirty, worn out, ill-fitting shoes — if you can stand the thought, much less the reality.

What is poverty? Poverty is getting up every morning from a dirty and illness-stained mattress — a hard, lumpy mattress. Sheets? There are no sheets. They have long since been used for diapers, for there are no real diapers here, either.

That smell? That other smell? You know what it is — plus sour milk and spoiled food. Sometimes it's mixed with the stench of onions cooked too often. Onions are cheap.

We're like dogs in that we live in a world of smells and we've learned to identify most of them without searching them out. There is the smell of young children who can't make it down that long path at night. There is the smell of the filthy mattress. There is the smell of food gone sour because the refrigerator

---

* From the files of the Office of Economic Opportunity.

doesn't work. I don't remember when the refrigerator did work. I only know it takes money to get it fixed. And there is the smell of garbage. I could bury it, but where do you get a shovel without money?

Poverty is being tired — dog tired all the time. I can't remember when I wasn't tired. When my last baby came, they told me at the hospital that I had chronic anemia caused by a poor diet, a bad case of worms, and the need for a corrective operation.

When they told me about my condition, I listened politely. The poor are always polite, you know. We can't afford to offend those who might decide to be big and give us something. The poor always listen, for there really isn't much we can say. If we were to say anything, it might prejudice somebody with a little money. What good would it do to say there is no money for iron pills, better food, or necessary medicine?

The idea of an operation is frightening even if you have the money required. If I had dared, I would have laughed. Who would have taken care of my children while I was in the hospital for a prolonged period?

The last time I left my children with their grandmother was when I had a job. I came home to find the baby covered with fly specks and wearing a diaper that had not been changed since I left. When the dried diaper was removed, bits of my baby's flesh were on it. My middle child was playing with a sharp piece of glass, and my oldest was playing alone at the edge of an unprotected lake. On my job I made $22 a week. A nursery school charges $20 a week for three children. So I had to quit my job.

Poverty is dirt. You may say, in your clean clothes and coming from your clean house, "Anybody can be clean." Let me explain housekeeping with no money. For breakfast, I give my children grits with no margarine, or cornbread made without eggs or oleo. For one thing, that kind of food doesn't use up many dishes. What dishes there are, I wash in cold water. No soap. Even the cheapest soap has to be saved for washing the old sheets I use for the baby's diapers.

Look at these cracked red hands. Once I saved up for two months to buy a jar of Vaseline for my hands and for the baby's diaper rash. When I had the money and went to buy the Vaseline, the price had gone up two cents, and I didn't have another two cents. Every day I have to decide whether I can bear to put these cracked, sore hands into that cold water and strong soap. Why don't I use hot water? It takes money to get something with which you can heat it. Hot water is a luxury. We don't have luxuries.

You would be surprised if I told you my age. I look twenty years older than I am; my back has been bent over tubs so long I can't stand up straight any more. I can't remember when I did anything but wash, but we're still dirty. I just can't seem to keep up with all the washing. Every night I wash every stitch my school-age child had on and just hope the clothes will be dry enough to wear when morning comes.

Poverty is staying up all night when it is cold to guard the one fire we have; one spark striking the newspaper we have on our walls would mean my sleeping children would die in the flames. In the summer, poverty is watching gnats and flies devour my baby's tears when he cries, which is most of the time. I've never been in an air-conditioned house. I've just heard folk talk about them. Our screens are torn, but we pay so little rent that I know it's foolish to even talk about getting them fixed. Poverty means insects in your food, in your nose, in your eyes, and crawling over you while you sleep. Poverty is children with runny noses, even in the summer. Paper handkerchiefs take money, and you need all your rags for other things. Antihistamines are for the rich.

Poverty is asking for help. Have you ever had to swallow what pride you had left and ask for help, knowing your children will suffer more if you don't get it? Think about asking for a loan from a relative, if that's the only way you can really understand asking for help.

I'll tell you how asking for help feels: You find out where the office is, the one from which paupers are supposed to get help. When you find it, you circle that block four or five times trying to get up nerve enough to go in and beg. Finally, the thought of your children's need and suffering pushes you through the door. Everybody is very busy and official. After an eternity, a woman comes out to you and you tell her you need help, and you force yourself to look at her.

She isn't the one you need to see. The first one never is. She sends you to see someone else and, after spilling your poverty and shame all over the desk, you find out this isn't the right office. Then you repeat the whole procedure. It doesn't get any easier.

You ask for help in two or three places, until you're sick of the whole procedure, but you're always told to wait. You are told why you have to wait but you don't really hear, because the dark cloud of shame and despair deafens you with its roar of recrimination.

Poverty is remembering — remembering quitting school in junior high school because the nice children from nice homes were so cruel about your clothes and your smell. (There have always been smells — you think you should have been a bloodhound.) I remember when I quit and the attendance teacher came to see my mother. She told him I was pregnant. I wasn't, but my mother knew they wouldn't make me go back to school if she told them that. She thought I could get a job and bring home some money. I had jobs off and on, but never long enough to earn much.

I remember mostly being married. I was so young. I'm still young, but you can't tell it. In another town, for a little while we had most of the things you have; a little house with lights, hot water and everything. Then my husband lost his job. For a little while there was some unemployment insurance, but soon all our nice things were repossessed and we moved back here — I was pregnant at the time. This house didn't look so bad when we first moved in. Every week it got worse, though. Nothing was ever fixed. Soon we didn't have any money at all.

My husband got a few odd jobs, but everything went for food — just as it does now. I'll never know how we lived through three years and three babies, but we did. After that last baby, I just plain destroyed my marriage. Would you want to bring another baby into this filth? I didn't, and birth-control measures take money. I knew the day my husband left that he wasn't coming back, but neither of us said anything. What was there to say? I hope he has been able to climb out of this mess somewhere. He never could hope to do it here, with us to drag him down.

It was after he left that I first asked for help. I finally got it: $78 a month for the four of us. That's all we'll ever get. That's why there is no soap, no medicine, no needles, no hot water, no aspirin, no hand cream, no shampoo — none of those things ever. And forever. I pay $20 a month rent. The rest goes for food: grits, cornmeal, rice, beans and milk.

Poverty is looking into a future colored only the blackest black. There is no hope. Your children wouldn't play with my children; you wouldn't allow it. My boys will someday turn to boys who steal to get what they need. I can already see them behind prison bars, but it doesn't bother me as it would you. They'll be better off behind prison bars than they would be behind the bars of my poverty and despair. They'll find the freedom of alcohol and drugs — the only freedom they'll ever know.

My daughter? She'll have a life just like mine, unless she's pretty enough to become a prostitute. I'd be smart to wish her dead already.

You say there are schools? Sure there are, but my children have no paper, no pencils, no crayons, no clothes, no anything worthwhile or useful. All they have is worms, pinkeye, infections of all sorts all the time. They aren't hungry, but they are undernourished. There are surplus commodity programs some places, I hear, but not here. Our county said it would cost too much. There is a school lunch program, but I have two children who are already too damaged for that to do them any good.

Yes, I know there are health clinics. They are in the towns, and I live eight miles from any town. I can walk that far, but my little children can't, and I can't carry them.

I have a neighbor who will take me to town when he goes, but he expects to be paid one way or another. No thanks; at least the hungry children I have are legitimate. You may know my neighbor. He is the large fellow who spends his time at the gas station, the barber shop, and the corner complaining loudly about the government spending money on the immoral mothers of illegitimate children.

Poverty is an acid that eats into pride until pride is burned out. It is a chisel that chips at honor until honor is pulverized. You might do something if you were in my situation — for a week or a month. Would you do it year after year, getting nowhere?

Even I can dream. I dream of a time when there is money — money for the right kind of food, for medicine, for vitamins, for a toothbrush, for hand cream, for a hammer and nails, for screens, for a shovel, for paint, for sheets, for needles, and thread and . . . but I know it's a dream, just like you know it's a dream when you see yourself as President.

Most, though, I dream of such things as not having wounded pride when I'm forced to ask for help. I dream for the peace of sincerely not caring any more. I dream of a time when the offices I visit for help are as nice as other government offices, when there are enough workers to get to you quickly, when those workers don't quit in defeat and despair just as poor folk quit hoping. I dream of the time when I have to tell my story just once each visit, to just one person. I'm tired of proving my poverty over and over and over.

I leave my despair long enough to tell you this: I did not come from another place, and I did not come from another time. I'm here, now, and there are others like me all around you.

Chapter Two

HUNGER

In America millions of federal dollars are given to farmers if they refrain from farming. Hogs are slaughtered, milk is washed down a sewer, and grain is left to rot. Senator-farmers, reaping huge federal subsidies, stoutly resist any attempt to curtail this practice. Often these same United States Senators have the most serious starvation in their own backyards.

Why does America permit this? In the past it has often been simply a matter of ignorance. However, the overwhelming facts have now been so widely disseminated that ignorance can no longer be considered a viable excuse. The findings of the McGovern Commission clearly document the tragic state of affairs existing in our country. The hunger Dr. Robert Coles reported nearly five years ago is still fact and still a cause for national shame.

The effects of hunger and malnutrition in the lives of our citizens is evident. When we can see, with little sympathy, the adult who, through sheer stupidity, eats himself into an early grave, we can no longer ignore the faces of the starving in America. To talk of America as a land of equal opportunity in one breath and to continue to be unconcerned about the hungry of America is the cruelest kind of deceit.

Estimates of top government officials place the cost of insuring an adequate diet for all Americans at approximately twelve billion dollars. Although this may seem a large amount at first glance, the long term gains which would be achieved for our society in terms of human resources make the cost seem remarkably small.

Starvation In the Affluent Society*

Joseph S. Clark

Gloria Palmer, a round-eyed, solemn-faced little girl of ten, stood shyly outside her slum home in Washington, D.C., and shifted her six-months-old baby brother from one arm to another, while two other tots leaned against her and stared up at the two United States Senators. Curiosity and childish bafflement were written across their faces. They did not know what Senators were or why they should be asking questions, nor did they recognize Senator Robert Kennedy or me. As we talked in front of the dilapidated and condemned tenements on Defrees Street, five blocks away could be seen the gleaming white dome of the Capitol.

I asked Gloria — one of eleven children of Wilhelmina Palmer — what she had eaten for lunch. "We didn't have any lunch," said Gloria quietly, and added, "But we have black-eyed peas for supper a lot." I asked her little brother, George, aged seven, "What did you have for lunch yesterday?" George replied, "Soup." "And what did you have for breakfast?" "Soup," George said.

A community action worker, who accompanied Senator Kennedy and me on this personal inspection of slums in the shadow of the Capitol, commented: "There are hundreds of others in

* *The Progressive* (October, 1967).
* Reprinted by permission of *The Progressive* (© 1967), The Progressive, Inc., Madison, Wisconsin.

this neighborhood who are hungry, kids and adults who get up in the morning hungry and who go to bed at night hungry. It's been that way ever since I've been here, years and years."

When Senator Kennedy remarked that Gloria should have been in school during this neighborhood visit of our Senate Subcommittee on Employment, Manpower and Poverty, my thoughts suddenly whirled back two weeks to another group of youngsters who were also hungry and also not in school.

This time the subcommittee, of which I serve as chairman, was walking along the dusty, sun-seared country roads of the Mississippi Delta. Here in ramshackle homes of one or two rooms holding families of eight and ten, we encountered children who were not sent to school by their mothers because they had no shoes. Later on, doctors suggested to us a more shocking reason: "bloated stomachs, chronic sores of the upper lip, and extreme lethargy — all tragic evidence of serious malnutrition."

In Belzoni, heart of the Delta, a mother of four told me that she and her brood had bologna sandwiches for breakfast and this would be the big meal of their day. Other times they have rice or grits, she told me in an infinitely tired voice, "but we never have any milk or fruit or fresh meat." Over and over again I was told that the staple diet for Belzoni's poor was beans, rice, margarine, lard, meal, peanut butter, raisins, powdered milk, and one can of meat for each person in the family per month. The can lasts, at the most, a week and a half.

The children we saw were visibly underweight, their bodies spotted with sores and untreated lesions.

Mrs. Ollie May Chapman and her nine children live in a tarpaper shack in Belzoni. On the day she was interviewed the family had gone without breakfast; for lunch they had soup made from a meat bone and cornmeal bread. For supper they would have beans — and a rare treat, a can of peaches.

We found a mother of fifteen children nursing a three-day-old child which she had delivered herself. There was no food in the house, she said, and no money. She didn't know what she would do.

Near Greenville, Mississippi, I came across a tumbledown collection of shack's ironically called Freedom City, housing the families of displaced plantation workers. Surviving, somehow, in this appalling squalor were forty-eight children who subsisted entirely on grits, rice, soybeans, and "whatever is donated," plus the customary one can of meat per month. Eggs, milk, and fruit juice, the mothers told me, were unknown.

There is no way in which you can prepare yourself for the overpowering effect of hunger and starvation seen close up. No matter how familiar you may be with the facts and figures of malnutrition, nothing can avert the feeling of stunned, disbelieving horror at the sight of little children with swollen bellies, shriveled limbs, and open sores that disfigure the small, bewildered faces and weakened bodies.

One reaches desperately for comparisons to give some semblance of reality to an experience that is essentially unreal and irrational. The mind rejects the evidence that innocent children *can and do* starve in this most abundant and fruitful of all nations, or go hungry in the Delta which contains 6 million acres of the richest land on the continent. The visitor reaches for analogies. Senator Kennedy remarked that what he saw on our visit to the Mississippi Delta was as bad as anything he encountered in Latin America. A former British Army doctor with extensive experience in Africa told us that what he saw in Mississippi was comparable only to what he had observed in primitive parts of Kenya. Another doctor who worked for the World Health Organization in Asia told me, "I've been in India and I've seen famine and starvation. What we have seen in Mississippi and places in the North is slow starvation."

Yes, the North, too, allows its citizens, including its children, to waste away with hunger and to starve. Hunger, we discovered, is no respecter of area or region. No state is free of hunger any more than any state is free of poverty and deprivation. There is hunger, for example, in prosperous Illinois, which admits that 1,281,100 people, or 12 percent of the state's population, have incomes below the poverty line.

The subcommittee recently reported that in a small Appalachian town, near the border between Virginia and Tennessee, five small children tore apart and devoured a chicken before it could be cooked. It was the first meat the family had eaten in three months.

"In the San Joaquin Valley of California," our report continued, "fifty yards off a seldom-traveled road, a migrant family of seven, the youngest child not yet two, were living in a pick-up truck abandoned by a small stream. They had had no breakfast and did not know where they would find food for lunch. In other years they could have fished, but the stream had dried up."

As such specific cases as these came increasingly to the attention of the subcommittee, we were struck by the discovery that these instances could not be projected against an overall picture of malnutrition and hunger in the United States. The fact is we simply do not know the extent or severity of malnutrition in this country today. Newspapermen were shocked when the U.S. Surgeon General told the subcommittee that we know more about malnutrition in Pakistan and other poor countries than in the United States. He said such studies have not been made in this country and, if they were to be made, he was not sure which agency should make them.

How vague our information is can be judged by the fact that the subcommittee was forced to report, after soliciting the best opinion available, that "estimates of the number of American citizens in serious need of food vary from as few as 400,000 to more than 4,000,000." Twelve years ago a federal study estimated that 23 percent of America's poor—those with incomes under $3,000—had "poor diets." In 1955 that meant 7,500,000 Americans had insufficiently nutritious diets.

Nor do we know with any degree of accuracy the minimum cost of an adequate diet. An Office of Economic Opportunity official told me a tentative conclusion had been reached that an average of $16 a month or $192 a year would provide one person with a "minimum low standard diet—enough to hold body and soul together."

On the basis of other figures compiled by the Department of Agriculture, it seemed more realistic to assume an annual minimum food cost per individual of $225, about twenty-one cents a meal.

Manifestly what is needed before the government can deal decisively with hunger and malnutrition is a comprehensive and incisive study of the problem. We must know the number of Americans who suffer from malnutrition and, next, what can be done to correct their inadequate diets.

Let us return to Mississippi because here surveys and studies have been made, and possibly they may provide clues to the nationwide dimensions of the hunger problem.

A study this year by the Department of Agriculture covered 509 poor families in two wealthy Delta counties. At least 60 percent of these families had diets providing less than two-thirds of the *minimum* dietary requirements recommended by the National Research Council. Moreover, these family diets were seriously deficient in milk, vegetables, and fresh fruits. The value of all the meals consumed by the average individual in the study was a miserable four dollars a week, or fifty-seven cents a day, including the foods distributed free by the federal government.

A spot-check study in seven Delta counties was made by the Mississippi Council on Human Relations and reported to us by its Executive Director, Kenneth L. Dean. Here are brief excerpts from the report:

> Using an economic standard, Mississippi is the poorest state in the republic. The fact that we receive more Office of Economic Opportunity poverty program funds per capita than any other state, and that during the month of March, 1967, 405,000 people received food assistance, indicate that there is a widespread problem of poverty that could, at any given moment, turn into acute hunger or a slow starvation if federal programs are not upgraded in keeping with population trends. . . .
>
> The most acute problem of hunger, and the most common situation, is the middle-aged mother, without a husband, in a small two-room shack, caring for somewhere between four and fifteen children. Most of the children will be of school age but many will not be attending school. . . .
>
> The diet of such a family usually consists of a breakfast of grits, molasses, and biscuit. For lunch the adults will eat nothing, and the children who are at home will be given a piece of bread and a drink of Kool-aid or water. The evening meal usu-

ally consists of boiled beans and corn bread. Sometimes boiled rice, dry peanut butter, or a canned meat substitute from the commodity program will supplement the evening meal.

These people, while not starving in the extreme sense of the word, are suffering from acute hunger. This hunger could be called starvation in that people's bodies actually are being denied proper sustenance, which causes the mortality rate of the [Negro] children to be much higher than that of whites, and which also shortens the life span of adults considerably. Medical doctors who work among these people say they never know the depth of their hunger for, from the time of birth on, they never have enough to eat.

Any consideration of hunger, in Mississippi or elsewhere, must take cognizance, as does the council's report, of the distribution of surplus foods. One-fifth of Mississippi's entire population is now being fed through the federal food distribution programs. But the too-seldom-recognized fact is that surplus foods were never intended to comprise full meals or adequate diets. Nevertheless, they have become almost the only source of food for hundreds of thousands of Americans. The meaning of this for nutrition and health can be perceived in the fact that the total value of the commodities distributed amounts to about $5 per person per month. They consist chiefly of flour, cornmeal, dry milk, and shortening. Only recently was the one can of meat per person per month added to the diet.

Appalling as this situation was, it became worse when a shift from surplus commodities to food stamps in just eight Mississippi counties in one year's time deprived 36,000 poor residents of their commodity allotments. The result simply had to be more hunger and more malnutrition since these people could not afford to buy food stamps to exchange for groceries.

By far the most impressive testimony on hunger was given to the Senate subcommittee by a group of six doctors who made a first-hand investigation of malnutrition and starvation in the Delta. Sponsored by the Field Foundation, the doctors comprised a distinguished panel of medical experts: Dr. Joseph Brenner, Medical Department, Massachusetts Institute of Technology; Dr. Robert Coles, Harvard University Health Service; Dr. Alan

Mermann, Department of Pediatrics, Yale University; Dr. Milton
J. E. Senn, Sterling Professor of Pediatrics, Yale University;
Dr. Cyril Walwyn, Medical Adviser to Friends of the Children
of Mississippi and a private practitioner in Mississippi; and
Dr. Raymond Wheeler, a private practitioner of Charlotte, North
Carolina.

Their report emerged as a unique document, unique in its
fusion of professional and humanitarian shock and profound
concern. Here is part of their findings on hunger among the
Delta's children:

> We saw children whose nutritional and medical condition
> we can only describe as shocking — even to a group of physicians
> whose work involves daily confrontation with disease and suffer-
> ing. In child after child we saw evidence of vitamin and mineral
> deficiencies; serious untreated skin infections and ulcerations;
> eye and ear diseases; also unattended bone diseases; the preva-
> lence of bacterial and parasitic diseases as well as severe anemia
> with resulting loss of energy and ability to lead a normally active
> life; diseases of the heart and lung — requiring surgery — which
> have gone undiagnosed and untreated; epileptic and other neu-
> rological disorders; severe kidney ailments that in other chil-
> dren would warrant immediate hospitalization; and finally, in
> boys and girls in every county we visited, obvious evidence of
> severe malnutrition, with injury to the body tissues — its mus-
> cles, bones, and skin as well as an associated psychological state
> of fatigue, listlessness, and exhaustion.
>
> We saw homes with children who are lucky to eat one meal
> a day — and that one inadequate so far as vitamins, minerals, or
> protein are concerned. We saw children who don't get to drink
> milk, don't get to eat fruit, green vegetables, or meat. They live
> on starches — grits, bread, Kool-aid. They are living under such
> primitive conditions that we found it hard to believe we were
> examining American children in the twentieth century.
>
> In some we saw children who are hungry and who are sick
> — children for whom hunger is a daily fact of life and sickness,
> in many forms, an inevitability. *We do not want to quibble over
> words, but "malnutrition" is not quite what we found, the boys
> and girls we saw were hungry — weak, in pain, sick, their lives
> are being shortened; they are, in fact, visibly and predictably*

losing their health, their energy, and their spirits. They are suf-
fering from hunger and disease and directly or indirectly they
are dying from them — which is exactly what "starvation"
means.

The charge of starvation was supported by all six of these eminent doctors.

In their individual testimony before the Senate Subcommittee, the doctors presented other observations and conclusions, some of them almost heartbreaking.

Dr. Wheeler: "Only one of the [Delta] families I visited ever had milk at all and this was reserved for 'the sickliest' ones. One mother summed up the question of diet in a single, poignant sentence: 'These children go to bed hungry and get up hungry and don't ever know nothing else in between.' Thin arms, sunken eyes, lethargic behavior, and swollen bellies were everywhere to be seen."

Dr. Brenner: "What is it that makes these Negro children so vulnerable to diseases that ordinarily are no longer considered killers in the United States? These children are vulnerable because their bodily resistance is so low they don't have ability to cope with infections the way healthy children have. The main cause of lack of resistance is malnutrition. The food available to them lacks the vital components that are necessary to build healthy bodies that can develop resistance against disease. . . . I would estimate that among the many families that I saw and I visited, with 150 to 160 children, at least three-quarters of them get less than the vital amount of animal protein per day—at least three-quarters, and I think I am being very conservative. Increasing evidence has come from different countries to suggest that infants both before birth and after birth, deprived of the kinds of food which are necessary for normal bodily growth, suffer not only visible damage to their bodies but also to the central nervous system, to the brain."

Dr. Coles: "I would like to speak briefly about the psychiatric aspect of my work. . . . I am describing in detail what it means for a child and his or her parents to be sick, more or less all the time, and hungry, more or less regularly. From all that one can learn, the aches and sores of the body become, for a child of four or five, more than a concrete physical factor of life; they bring in the child's mind a reflection of his worth and a judgment upon him and his family by the outside world. They ask themselves and others what they have done to be kept from the food they want or what they have done to deserve the pain they feel.

"In my experience with families in the Delta, their kind of life can produce a form of withdrawn, sullen behavior. I have seen some of the families I knew in the South go North and carry with them that state of mind and I am now working with them in Boston. They have more food, more welfare money, and, in the public hospitals of the Northern city, certain medical services. But one sees how persistently sickness and hunger in children live on into adults who doubt any offer, mistrust any goodness or favorable turn of events.

"I fear that we have among us now in this country hundreds of thousands of people who have literally grown up to be and learned to be tired, fearful, anxious, and suspicious. . . . The children need food, the kind of food that will enable their bones to grow, their blood to function as it should, their vital organs to remain healthy, and their minds to stay alert. It is inconceivable to us that children at this stage of American history, and in the context of American wealth, continue to live like this in Mississippi, in Alabama, in Kentucky, in West Virginia, in the Southwest, and, indeed, carry this condition of life to all of our Northern cities."

Later I asked Dr. Coles, a vital young psychiatrist who has not become insensitized by repeated trips into the most poverty-stricken areas of the Deep South and Appalachia, how many children suffering from malnutrition live in the Delta region today.

"There is no way, at present, of knowing for certain," he replied. "There are thousands and thousands of children in the Delta we didn't see, out of sight, out of reach, out of mind, out of access to white doctors and Negro doctors. There must be between 50,000 and 100,000 children suffering from malnutrition in the Delta."

Dr. Coles agreed on the use of the word "starvation" rather than "malnutrition." "The kind of starvation we observed," he said, "is the kind of starvation in which the body is slowly consuming itself. The body is victimized by diseases which definitely can shorten life. We saw severe malnutrition, hunger and starvation in the sense that the body is irretrievably going downhill."

I am convinced from what I saw that among the great number of Negroes who have moved from the Deep South to Northern ghettos are some who knew starvation in the South as children, and that this bitter experience makes some of them potential recruits for the riots in the cities.

I wish to reemphasize, as would the doctors, that hunger, malnutrition, and slow starvation are not confined to the Deep South nor to any other part of the country. There is, certainly, widespread hunger and malnutrition in all the Negro ghettos, north and south.

Washington, D.C., for example, is no better nor any worse than any other American city, although undoubtedly, as the center of federal government, it should be better. One-third of the population of the nation's capital exists at little more than subsistence level.

Under the District of Columbia's Headstart program, for example, 4,200 children recently received physical examinations. Between 40 and 50 percent of these youngsters were found to have low hemoglobin counts, a condition (when not caused by infection) reflecting a food deficiency which produces nutritional anemia.

Deficient diets among Washington children are also indicated in the School Free Lunch Program which provides free lunches in elementary and secondary schools *only on application by the family, certifying need*. Nationally, a total of 11 percent of all schoolchildren receive free school lunches, but in Washington they are provided to 51 percent of all school youngsters.

Another index of deficient diets in the nation's capital is found in Public Assistance payments, which provide a maximum of $417 a month for a family of thirteen, including $228 for food, which comes to nineteen cents a meal for each member of the family.

The subcommittee's disclosures—preliminary as they are—of hundreds of thousands, perhaps millions, of hungry Americans have had two early results. The first was an unexpected public response; the second was the subcommittee's success in effecting a quick change in the Department of Agriculture's food stamp policies and in moving emergency legislation through the Senate.

Perhaps we should have anticipated the public's warm, sympathetic response to the revelations of hunger, but actually members of the subcommittee were surprised by the letters and telephone calls they received from concerned citizens. Some of the letters contained checks; mostly the writers inquired (as did the callers) where money and collections of food and clothing could be sent. Frequently the letters combined expressions of heartfelt solicitude with indignant comments on the affluent society that allowed penury and hunger to persist.

The way in which the food stamp program operated, particularly the cash payments required of poor families, was seen by the subcommittee as a major obstacle to alleviating hunger. Time and again, in Mississippi and in Washington, the subcommittee was told that many families could not afford the $2 per person a month that would buy them desperately needed food stamps worth much more when exchanged for commodities. A family of six, for example, would have to pay $12 a month for coupons exchangeable for $72 worth of food. Many families, we were told, went "months on end without seeing $12 all together."

Finally, after an impatient exchange of letters between the subcommittee and the Secretary of Agriculture Orville Freeman, and appeals to the White House, the Department of Agriculture was induced to cut the cost of food stamps from $2 to fifty cents. This meant that the family of six that previously paid $12 for $72 worth of food would now pay $3. With other members of the subcommittee, I hope that even the fifty cents charge can be eliminated and stamps be made available to the needy free of charge.

In addition, the subcommittee persuaded Sargent Shriver's Office of Economic Opportunity to institute an emergency $1,000,000 four-month Food Stamp Loan Program in twenty counties in seven Southern states. This provides the needy with cash loans ranging from $2 to $12 a month, depending on the size of the family. It now makes possible the purchase of food stamps by thousands of families that previously could not afford them. By the end of the year it is expected that 30,000 families (with an average of four to a family) will have obtained OEO loans for food stamps in these Deep South counties.

Emergency legislation was the next step, and for once the normally laggard machinery of the U.S. Senate moved with dispatch. On Friday, July 21, Senator John Stennis, Mississippi Democrat, introduced a bill proposing a $10,000,000 appropriation to provide, on an emergency basis, "food and medical services to any individual in any state whenever such action is required to prevent the loss of such individual's life or to avoid suffering caused by lack of food or medical attention." By late afternoon, several other Senators and I, all members of the Labor and Public Welfare Committee, had joined as co-sponsors of the bill and had pledged the speediest possible action on the proposal.

On the following Tuesday the bill was unanimously approved by the full committee but not before the $10,000,000 appropriation was increased to $25,000,000 for the first year and $50,-000,000 for the second, and an amendment added to initiate the first comprehensive study in the nation's history "of the incidence and location of serious hunger and malnutrition and health problems incident thereto...." The bill sailed through the Senate the next day without a single dissenting vote.

I am hopeful that the new war on poverty legislation—which includes additional funds of $2.8 billion approved by the Senate Committee on Labor and Public Welfare for a series of improving amendments to the existing Economic Opportunity Act— will make a major contribution toward the abolition of poverty and hunger. By strengthening the Job Corps, the Neighborhood Youth Corps, adult work-training, aid to small business, community action programs, assistance to migrant workers, rural loans, Headstart and VISTA—by making these programs more effective, I believe we can do much to raise American living standards and begin the long-overdue eradication of poverty, hunger, and malnutrition.

As the long hot summer of 1967, with its unprecedented civil disorders, bloodshed, and looting, recedes into history, the nation and its leaders find themselves reassessing their goals and priorities. Remembering the devastated neighborhoods, the burned-out homes and shops, in nearly thirty cities across the country, I found the words of the philosopher Seneca, 2,000 years ago, echoing meaningfully down to our day: "A hungry people listens not to reason, nor cares for justice, nor is bent by any prayers."

Now, as never before, reason and justice dictate that we devote our purpose and our nation's resources to the goal that there shall no longer be hungry people in an America of over-flowing abundance.

Malnutrition and Learning*

Merrill S. Read

Increasing knowledge of the effects of malnutrition, combined with the social consciousness of the 1960's, has turned national attention to the nutritional status of Americans. Growing evidence that nutrition may affect intellectual and behavioral as well as physical growth has stimulated efforts to determine the extent of malnutrition in the United States and to assess its long-term impact.

Experts disagree about the extent of malnutrition in America partly because of a confusion of terms. Malnutrition is not synonymous with hunger but, of course, may result from long periods of insufficient food. Hunger can be easily and immedi-

ately relieved with food; malnutrition requires prolonged rehabilitation and may leave lasting effects.

Here malnutrition is defined as a state in which an individual
lacks one or more nutrients to the extent that specific symptoms
and conditions appear (such as anemia, goiter, rickets or vitamin deficiencies) or retardation in physical development occurs.
Severe malnutrition refers to two types of diseases resulting
from prolonged protein and/or calorie insufficiency in early
childhood: marasmus results from severe restriction of food
intake—particularly of calories—from birth or shortly after
and is manifest in wasting of the tissues and severe growth
retardation. Kwashiorkor, a result of inadequate protein intake,
occurs most often when the child changes from breast or bottle
milk to foods high in starch but low in protein. It produces
extreme stunting of growth, water retention, skin sores, and
discoloration of the hair to red or blond. Both diseases cause
death if untreated.

Malnutrition is most often associated with poverty. Yet,
determining its effects on a given individual is extremely difficult since many other factors influence human growth and
behavioral development, including an individuals innate potential, his health status, the conditions in which he lives, and
his relationships with his family and the rest of society.

The National Nutrition Survey, begun in 1968 and being
carried out by the Department of Health, Education, and Welfare, is the first comprehensive effort to assess the nutritional
status of the U.S. population. Preliminary results have been
reported on the study of 12,000 people of all ages, randomly
selected in poverty pockets in two States and several smaller
areas; ultimately the sample will include pockets in 10 or more
States. Because of the poverty orientation of these studies, the
majority of people examined were Negroes, although other
ethnic groups were included.

The survey found an unexpectedly high prevalence of symptoms associated with malnutrition. Four to five percent of the
people examined exhibited symptoms sometimes associated with

---

* *American Education.* (December 1969).

severe malnutrition, although very few cases of marasmus or kwashiorkor were found. One-third of the children under six years old and 15 percent of the total sample population were found to have low blood hemoglobin levels diagnosed as anemia or iron deficiency.

About 17 percent—nearly 2,000 of those examined—showed abnormally low protein levels in their blood. Vitamin D, necessary for the absorption of calcium and the normal development of bones, was found to be lower than normal in the blood of 58 children under six years of age, and 18 cases of rickets were diagnosed. Deficiencies in vitamins A and C and in iodine were also found in a significant number of persons examined.

Other surveys carried out in the United States generally confirm the existence among the poor of the nutritional problems found in the National Survey. One study compared 558 preschool children from several economic levels in 20 counties in Mississippi. The 210 children from poor families were found to eat fewer calories and to take in significantly less protein, calcium, and vitamin C than the other groups; they also were considerably smaller and lighter physically.

Surveys have shown that the average North American Indian family of five persons, living on a reservation, attempts to survive on an annual income below $2,000. A study of 195 Apache children between one and six years old disclosed that one-third of them had anemia and deficiencies in vitamins A and C. Virtually all 165 children examined in one clinic had dental disease; half the cases were described as severe. In another group of 126 families, marked growth retardation was seen in children through age five years. Cases of severe malnutrition in children have also been found on Navajo reservations in the Southwest.

The results of these surveys are preliminary and in many cases cannot be directly compared. However, in the absence of complete national statistics, these studies suggest that multiple deficiencies of specific nutrients occur in varying degrees and in higher-than-expected proportions among poor people. A major factor contributing to the poor nourishment of infants is the decline of breast feeding, combined with inadequate information about food substitutes and poor sanitary conditions in the use of alternate foods.

The consequences of malnutrition depend on the time in the life of the individual when nutritional deficits occur, as well as on their severity and duration. The brain may be damaged by various influences during the period of fastest growth, which in human beings occurs from about five months before to about 10 months after birth. At the end of the first year the brain has achieved approximately 70 percent of its adult weight, and by the end of the second year, it has practically completed its growth.

The brain grows both by increase in the number of cells and by increase in the side of each cell. Experiments with rats, made by Myron Winick of the Cornell University Medical College in New York, show that severe malnutrition during the period of cell division permanently reduces the total number of cells despite subsequent nutritional rehabilitation. Severe food restriction later during the growth period may reduce cell size during the period of starvation, but the cells retain the ability to enlarge with increased feeding.

Obviously, similar studies cannot be done with human infants. However, the brains of infants who died of marasmus in Chile were found by Dr. Winick to have only 40 percent of the expected number of cells when compared with the brains of infants who died from accidents. Severe malnutrition in a pregnant woman probably affects the unborn child by reducing the nutrients available to it for normal cell growth. Also, severe malnutrition during the first six months of the infant's life further reduces the number of brain cells the baby will develop. The timing of nutritional deprivation, therefore, is crucial.

Although information from experiments with animals cannot be applied directly to humans, who are infinitely more complicated, it can point the way to possible consequences for man. Rats and pigs fed severely restricted diets during periods of fastest brain growth and then later fed good diets have shown changes in behavior as well as in the size and composition of their brains. The animals cannot learn as fast as their normal littermates, cannot unlearn a task they have finally mastered, and tend to over-react in an agitated and irritable way when exposed to unpleasant situations.

In a pioneer study begun in 1955 in South Africa, investigators compared a group of 20 severely malnourished Negro infants, mostly aged 10 months to two years, with a second group of better nourished babies matched for race, age, sex, and low socioeconomic class. Eleven years later the severely malnourished children displayed significantly smaller head sizes and much lower intellectual achievement on various test measures than did the second group. Although their greater emotional and social deprivation may have affected the first group's test performance, the implications of long-lasting effects of malnutrition on mental development could not be ignored.

Another important early study was done by Joaquin Cravioto, currently head of the department of nutrition, Hospital Infantil de Mexico, on 20 Guatemalan preschool children who had been hospitalized for severe malnutrition in earlier childhood and had recuperated. Here Dr. Craviotor found that intellectual development was related to the age of the child at the time of affliction and to the duration of the malnutrition: events during the first six months of life appeared most critical for later normal development. For the first three years of their lives these children matched in all ways except for the malnutrition. With time, some of the differences narrowed between the groups, except in cases in which the malnutrition occurred very early in ilfe.

Recently Ernesto Pollitt, assistant professor of psychology at Yale, critically reviewed eight investigations — made in underdeveloped countries and completed in the last six years — in which children hospitalized with severe protein-calorie malnutrition were observed after recovery. Overall, the results suggested that kwashiorkor was not necessarily associated with permanent intellectual damage, at least if the child was older than 12 months when the condition began. Dr. Pollitt concluded that a child who suffers from kwashiorkor after an otherwise healthy early development seems to have a fair chance of recovering his full intellectual potential.

Children suffering from marasmus, on the other hand, were found to be more likely to have intellectual damage, probably because the brain grows faster during the early months of life when marasmus strikes. Marasmus might develop gradually from birth, increasingly debilitate the infant, and limit his responsiveness to his surroundings, especially his mother. As the child's responsiveness decreases, the mother may become disheartened and transfer her attention to other healthier children in the family. Thus, the marasmic child seems more likely to be permanently impaired because of his longer exposure to poor diet and multiple adverse environmental factors.

In Chile, Fernando B. Monckeberg, head of pediatrics at the University of Chile Medical School in Santiago, studied three groups of urban preschool children: a middle-class well nourished group, a lower-class group participating in a nutritional supplementation program, and a group of lower class malnourished children. He found the last group performed significantly poorer on tests of intellectual ability even though their environment was similar to that of the second group. The first two groups performed essentially alike, despite their environmental differences. In this study, poor nutrition appeared to be associated with poor test performance.

Studying an impoverished area more closely, Dr. Monckeberg examined 150 preschool children and their mothers. From tests, he found poor intellectual performance to be highly associated with smaller head size and low protein diets of the children. After evaluating the mothers' intellectual abilities, he could also relate the low maternal performance with the children's poor nutritional conditions and poor intellectual performance. Thus, the interrelation between inheritance, social deprivation, and intellectual ability remained unresolved.

Although kwashiorkor and marasmus occur infrequently in the United States, cases are now being seen in hospitals that serve large lower-income populations. Peter Chase and colleagues at the University of Colorado Medical Center in Denver have reported a long-term follow-up study of 19 infants admitted to a hospital over a two-year period for treatment of marasmus or kwashiorkor. They compared these infants with another group which, so far as possible, were distinguished from them only by their state of nutrition. The investigators found that although all the children in the study showed an adequate growth rate three and one-half years after treatment, the malnourished children failed to catch up to the second group mentally or physically.

The researchers concluded that the duration of malnutrition in the first year of life of these infants correlated with their physical and mental development at the age of about four and one-half years when the children were studied. Examination of the family records showed that the mothers of the malnourished infants were under particular emotional and economic stress at the time of their infants' malnutrition, and that home conditions were especially bad. Furthermore, a primary cause of the poor nutritional condition of these infants was family disorganization, probably influenced by poverty and lack of education. In one case, an infant was left in the hands of her five-year-old sister. Since these social problems also may influence intellectual development, the effects of malnutrition alone are somewhat clouded in this study.

There are other conditions that tend to decrease learning experiences and possibly affect subsequent intellectual development. Children hospitalized with protein-calorie malnutrition may have experienced a form of social isolation in the period immediately preceding hospitalization. On top of this, opportunities for social contact frequently are reduced in the hospital rehabilitation ward. The child's fear of the new hospital environment also may inhibit his responses to learning opportunities. Pertinent recent studies have shown that social isolation may reduce the size and number of cells in rat brain much the same as malnutrition.

The evidence strongly supports the conclusion that early severe malnutrition is associated with intellectual impairment. However, carefully-planned studies are needed to determine whether any effects are due solely to malnutrition or to the unique constellation of environmental factors surrounding the malnourished hospitalized child who has most often been the subject for these studies.

Another major question concerns the effects of mild to moderate malnutrition on intellectual growth. These levels of undernutrition do not necessarily imperil survival, and hospitalization is not normally required, but they may cause growth retardation. Here there are few studies upon which to base a judgment, but the effects, if any, would certainly be expected to be less than for protein-calorie malnutrition. Furthermore, the interplay between social, medical, genetic, and nutritional variables might be expected to play a more prominent role.

In an eight-year study of Mexican children, investigators found that intellectual performance at the time of entry into school appeared to be related to the child's history of malnutrition. After the children spent four to five years in school, however, this relationship disappeared, and differences in performance appeared to be related more closely to socioeconomic conditions and regularity of school attendance.

Hence, iron deficiency anemia is the most frequently observed nutritional problem among infants, preschool, and young children. Its effects upon learning and behavior have not been systematically investigated. One study of 28 children under the age of three who were admitted to an American hospital with iron deficiency has been reported. The subjects were matched with a group not having anemia. A year after discharge from the hospital, the children who had had anemia were found to have more illnesses, more feeding difficulties, and more behavioral problems than those in the other group. The investigators attributed the behavioral deficits to parental failure and family disintegration rather than to nutritional insufficiency.

A key problem in determining whether malnutrition, disease, or the social environmental factors of poverty have the greatest effect on mental development hinges on the timing of the testing. Intellectual and behavioral measurements are best made in middle childhood, whereas the nutritional insult, if it has an effect, probably occurs in infancy. Long term studies monitoring nutritional intake and behavior development are essential.

A study that may provide some answers is now being done in Guatemala where many people still live in small, isolated villages, subsist on an inadequate diet, and till the overworked fields of their ancestors. Without adequate medical care many babies die before their first birthday, and those who survive are short and undeveloped. In the villages under study, all participants receive heretofore unavailable medical care with special attention given to pregnant women, infants, and young children. The villages are studied in pairs so that they are as much alike as possible on socio-economic, public health, cultural, and other bases. Each village in a pair receives added stimulation through a carefully planned visitation and examination program. One village in each pair also receives a specially designed nutritional supplement. Thus the investigators hope to define the effects of better nutrition as they follow the growth and development of the children over the first seven years of life.

Up to now it has been generally assumed that intellectual deficits would be proportional to the degree of malnutrition imposed. On the other hand, it is also possible that there may be a level of malnutrition in infancy below which neurological structures are so altered that retarded intellectual development is irreversible. Above this threshold, however, undernutrition would have no serious consequences for neurological development itself. Genetic endowment and sociological factors surrounding malnutrition would then be expected to exert increasingly significant effects on intellectual ability.

Those who have worked with undernourished or hungry children know that they exhibit behavioral alterations. These include apathy, lethargy, inability to pay attention, and perhaps, overconcern about food to such a degree that responses to classroom stimuli do not occur. A child in such condition no longer meets the expectations of his family or teachers. He begins to live in a world of his own and may seek recognition to gain attention by ways that disrupt learning experiences.

Learning is increasingly recognized as progressing in stages, each stage becoming a foundation for the next. By not responding to early stimulation, the child gradually becomes unable to benefit from "normal" experiences at a later period. He fails to learn, not because the genetic potential or neurological structures are absent, but because he lacks the experiential foundation. Improved nutrition alone will not correct this deficit. Neither will improved educational opportunities by themselves. Both must be provided in a coordinated program to develop the child's potential.

Foremost among the problems requiring resolution is the developing of a battery of tests that can measure the behavioral and social variables involved and that are applicable to varied social groups. These tests need to be addressed to the changes that we now suspect are related to malnutrition. It is hoped that they will detect those low levels of change that might be expected under less severe nutritional conditions.

Because firm conclusions can be drawn that malnutrition per se is the cause of mental subnormality, carefully designed studies will be required to clarify the role of parents and of the social and environmental factors that accompany malnutrition. Because research cannot at this time give an unequivocal or complete answer to the question of what effect malnutrition has on intellectual development is no reason to delay programs for improving the nutritional status and eating practices of mothers and infants. Information demonstrating the benefits of good nutrition in improved health and physical growth already justify such efforts.

Hunger In America*

Charles Upton Lowe, M.D.

The limited educational mission of the Committee on Nutrition has changed. It has broadened to include a concern with the whole fabric and quality of American life to the extent that these relate to the care and nurture of our children. It is our conviction that nutrition is the key to the normal development of infants and children. In effect, the quality and quantity of

---

* U.S. Senate Select Committee on Nutrition and Human Needs, November 1969.

nutrition given during the first two to four years of life may have the effect of programming the individual for all the years of his life. Malnutrition during the last trimester of pregnancy and, certainly during the first months of life, may seriously compromise ultimate intellectual achievement. Experience in developing countries has indicated that the period of greatest nutritional risk is during the second to fifth year of life. These observations reflect the fact that in most evolving nations breast feeding is practiced for the first twelve or fourteen months of life and, therefore, nutrition is sound during this period. It is an error, however, to assume that danger does not exist earlier in life. In this country, among both impoverished and economically more advanced families, breast feeding is practiced to a decreasing extent. Under these circumstances, when the infant is fed by bottle very early in life, malnutrition from inappropriate feeding becomes possible even during the first months of life. The earlier malnutrition exists, the more devastatingly it impinges on growth and development.

We now have unambiguous evidence from several sources of the following facts:

1. When a fetus receives inadequate nutrition in utero, the infant is born small, the placenta of his mother contains fewer cells than normal to nourish him and his growth will be compromised.

2. When an infant undergoes severe nutritional deprivation during the first months of life, his brain fails to synthesize protein and cells at normal rates and consequently suffers a decrease as great as twenty percent in the cell number.

3. During the last trimester of pregnancy, protein synthesis by the brain is proceeding at a very rapid rate. Immediately upon delivery, this rapid rate decreases, although it still continues at a greater pace than at later times of life. In animals, this sharp decrease in protein synthesis immediately after birth occurs in both full term and premature animals. The decrease in protein synthesis occurring in premature animals in all probability also occurs in premature human infants. If we can extend animal observations to the human situation, we have a logical explanation for one of the most distressing concomitants

of prematurity; when very small at birth as many as fifty percent of prematurely born infants grow to maturity with an
intellectual competence significantly below that which would
be expected when compared with siblings and even with age peers.

4. Severe malnutrition suffered during childhood effects
learning ability, body growth, rate of maturation, ultimate size
and if prolonged, productivity.

These factors clarify our concept of the crucial importance
of nutrition at certain critical times during the growth cycle
of the brain and body of infants and children. The presence of
malnutrition during the first 5 years of life constitutes a danger
not only to the individual child but, also, when this exists among
a significant segment of our population, to our nation as a whole.
We cannot afford to let millions of children grow to adult life
compromised in intellect because we, in this rich land, have
failed to feed them. Our goal must be the total elimination of
malnutrition for we can tolerate nothing less.

May I now call your attention to the interrelation between
certain economic and medical realities. Almost 10.5 million children in this country grow up in families living in poverty. The
presence of poverty implies a family income insufficient to purchase many of the essentials of life. Unfortunately, food is one
of the essentials which is unavailable. In families living in poverty there is a far higher rate of infant mortality than in more
economically well-to-do families. In fact, a high infant mortality
rate may be the hallmark of poverty in the U.S.A. In addition,
the rate of premature births is also far higher, in some cases
two or three times higher than it is in more well-to-do families.
Finally, the prevalence of intellectual compromise and even mental deficiency may be from three to five times as frequent in children of families living in poverty. In effect, malnutrition, high
infant mortality and prematurity rates and high levels of mental
deficiency coexist as a constellation of abnormalities that are
most frequent among our families living in poverty. In addition,
poverty appears to have a predilection for families with children
and the presence of children within these families tends to perpetuate poverty by limiting the occupational options of the parents and educational opportunities of the children. One third of

all families in the United States with four or more children live in poverty.

It is not the povery per se, which must be of concern to this Committee, but rather, the fact that poverty carries with it a variety of social and economic disabilities. We have a sequence of aberrations, each of which feeds upon the others. This morbid chain must be broken. In my opinion the most readily accessible link is also the most critical. Were we to ensure that infants, children and pregnant mothers of this country receive adequate nutrition, we would interrupt the cycle and remodel the future. Infant mortality and prematurity rates would decrease. With this there would come to our children improved growth and development, certainly of body and probably of intellect. Educational accomplishment and achievement would improve and with this, economic status would rise.

I would like to make some further generalizations regarding nutrition in infants and children in this country. In contrast to the situation in less developed countries, an increasingly large proportion of infants and children in America are totally dependent, virtually from birth until well into the second year of life, upon manufactured food products. Manufactured formulas and manufactured infant and baby foods have become the major source of nutrition, even among those living on the verge of poverty. Under these circumstances, a special responsibility devolves to the manufacturers of these products. If significant errors in manufacturing procedure, composition or content of these foods occur, a year's crop of babies may be permanently damaged; if the aberration remains undetected for long, a whole generation may be injured. This special responsibility is well recognized and fulfilled by the relevant industries. But I believe it important that federal regulatory agencies maintain proper surveillance so that no damage can occur to this totally dependent population, America's infants and children. . . .

. . . .

In this age of superlatives we have become inured to descriptions of affluence and privation, opulence and poverty. It becomes difficult to winnow the hard statistic from the superficial impression. Under these circumstances, the establishment of realistic goals for political or personal action becomes hazardous.

From several sources we learn that significant malnutrition exists in our land, but many of us have not examined the issue seriously because of the origin of the reports. Too often these reports appear to be self serving. They arise as newspaper headlines or press releases emanating from those with a political investment in the subject. In addition, we find it hard to believe that privation so degrading and enervating can exist in this land of wealth and power. Yet we have a responsibility to examine this national issue critically. To the extent that each of us operates within the public or private sector, our action and opinion impinge upon the formation of public policy.

Let us examine the interrelations between nutrition, child care, and public policy and the evidence that these are related. We must inquire whether or not all the children of our land are adequately fed, and whether they receive sufficient medical care. We must also examine the interrelations between these two aspects of child health and the extent to which existing programs meet identified needs. The answers arising from analysis of these questions become relevant to the economic future of this country. We must review certain aspects of current economic theory and relate these to the nurture of our children. Child health must be scrutinized within the context of poverty, and the implications of povery. The impact of poverty on the future of our children must be evaluated. . . .

. . . .

The question we must ask ourselves is whether the children of our country now reared in poverty and deprived of an adequate diet will mature and become employable or unemployable. It takes no great jump in reasoning to conclude that the three million unemployed to which both President Johnson and John Tebbel referred came from the ranks of those who as children had been reared in disadvantaged environments.

To examine this problem we must explore the economic status of the families in which our children are reared; the evidence available that they get enough to eat, the hazards of malnutrition, and the implications that derive from these data.

First, let us examine the nature and scope of poverty. A recent publication of the OEO defines this group.

TABLE 1. THE POOR IN MILLIONS

	White	Nonwhite	Total
All ages			34.3
Children:			
Under 6 years	3.5	2.3	5.8
6 to 15 years	5.0	3.1	8.1
Total	8.5	5.4	13.9

NOTE. — 40 percent of our poor are children.

Source: "Dimensions of Poverty 1964," a publication from the Office of Economic Opportunity, October 1965.

"In March 1965, about 12 million households comprising thirty-four million persons were living on cash incomes insufficient to buy goods and services vital to health. Measured by the reports of 1964 cash incomes to the Census Bureau, these—based on a sliding scale of cash incomes allowing for family size and the ages of family members—are *The Poor,* averaging, on these incomes, at most, seventy cents a day per person for food, and choosing, among hard alternatives, which needs may be endured and which must be satisfied.

"Almost seventy percent of the poor where white; eighty-seven percent did not live on farms; forty-seven percent (over half of those not on farms) lived inside the metropolitan boundaries of areas containing cities of 50,000 population or more. As nearly as can be determined, cities, large and small, contain about fifty-five percent of all these poor. The rest spreads thinly like a retreating nerve network over the hamlet traces of past and dying industry, mining, lumbering, transportation, and farming, with rural nonfarm poverty outnumbering farm poverty two to one."

Of the fifty-eight million children in our country under fifteen years of age, 13.9 million, or 24%, live in poverty, the majority in 6.8 million family groups. The households of the poor account for only 11% of those still in high school and 32% of high school dropouts. (5) Excluding those over 65 from the calculation, 48% of the population of the poverty group comprises those under fifteen years of age, and 40% of all families living in poverty have children under six years of age. In contrast, only 30% of the national population is under fifteen years of age. Poverty has a predeliction for families with children and the presence of children within these families tends to perpetuate poverty by limiting the occupational options of the parents. One-third of all families with four or more children live in poverty.

TABLE 2. U.S. FOOD CONSUMPTION

	United States 1965	Great Britain 1962	Netherlands 1960
Pounds per person per year	1,280	1,395	1,289
Kcal per day	[1](3,000)	3,190	2,975
Kcal per pound of food	855	845	845

† Estimated.
Sources: The New Information Please Almanac Atlas and Year Book 1966; Bourne, G. H., World Review and Dietetics.

The average person in the United States consumes 1280 pounds of food per year and spends $435 to purchase it. (6) According to the OEO, the person living in poverty spends less than $255 per year on food, or a bit more than one-half of the national average (4). If we equate dollars to calories, we can calculate that $255 provides purchasing power for only 1680 calories per day per person. This is at best an approximation and its implications must be weighted to allow for the age distribution of those living in poverty and for the fact that many living in rural poverty grow some of their own food. The contribution of this portion of their diet to a national summation cannot be measured. Neither does this estimate include the direct contribution of food by government at all levels. The poor, in contrast to the rest of the population, spend a larger percent of their available income on food, more than thirty percent in contrast to less than twenty-five percent, buy within a restricted market and the food they purchase costs more than it does when bought by the affluent.

We must remember, however, that poverty is much more than a lack of cash. It is a way of life, all pervading, crushing, immobilizing, and destructive. It is self-perpetuating, and infectious, spreading through regions like an infectious illness. And it is cruel, enervating, and dehumanizing.

Performance of individuals has a way of falling between the lattice and chinks of statistics, and we must seek more direct evidence that poverty in this country is associated with a significant incidence of malnutrition. A national survey currently in progress will provide hard facts. Until these are available, we are left with only indirect evidence. First we have the anecdotal evidence. Kwashiorkor (Profound protein-calorie malnutrition of childhood) has been identified in isolated instances in two hospitals in New York, one in Cleveland, Rochester, and Seattle. We have no means to establish prevalence in these communities or in others.

Next we have the newspaper evidence. Much of this is flamboyant and hysterical but probably all has some basis in fact. An investigative committee of the Citizens Crusade Against Poverty reported that malnutrition was not uncommon in certain counties of South Carolina. (7) A physician gave testimony that he had seen "large numbers" of preschool children with some degree of Kwashiorkor, and a lay person told the committee that she had seen cases where children starved to death. South Carolina is the only state in the Southeast that does not participate in the Federal Government's direct Commodity Distribution Program.

The publicity given the non-governmental survey of malnutrition in Mississippi served to alert the country to this problem, though the reliability of the report has been questioned. Nevertheless, after the Senate passed the Stennis Bill which was to provide for Food and Medical Services on an emergency basis and support a nutrition survey, the New York Times commented editorally: "The poor, underdeveloped countries aren't the only ones with a hunger problem. Most Americans were surprised and shocked to learn during a Senate subcommittee's hearings

. . . that thousands in poverty areas of this country suffer from serious malnutrition and lack of medical care." (8)

What direct evidence do we have of malnutrition? A recently reported nutrition survey, conducted in Columbus, Ohio, gives some incidence data. (9) The preschool children living in three groups of families were studied; two were in the lowest economic quartile with mean incomes of $775 and $1,050/year, and one was in the second quartile with a mean annual family income of $1,525. Thirteen, or eleven percent of the 146 children examined had daily intakes during the period of study of less than 80 Kcal/kilo, a value probably well below the ideal. If this can be translated to encompass all the disadvantaged in our land, 1.5 million children are similarly deprived. . . .

.   .   .   .

Almost 20 percent of infant mortality is directly related to prematurity or immaturity at birth. In the last year about 7 percent of all births were premature, almost 280,000 infants. In a recent publication by the National Center for Health Statistics, it was stated that: "The causes of infant deaths in the United States are largely concentrated in five groups which account for three-fourths of all infant deaths—yet among these categories there are hidden associations which are not evident from the statistics. The thread of prematurity and/or immaturity runs through a number of these causes." (13) Eleanor Hunt summarized the problem as follows: "Much newborn mortality could be prevented if measures to sustain pregnancy 36 weeks could be applied successfully." (14)

There seems to be no question, therefore, among those who have studied the statistics, that within the confines of the problems of premature birth and its prevention lies one solution to the major national disgrace found in our infant mortality figures. The question we must ask is whether this relates in any definable way to nutrition. The answer appears to be "yes." For example, in a national conference on Infant Mortality, E. W. Page, Chairman of the Department of Obstetrics and Gynecology at the University of California at San Francisco, after reviewing 12,000 premature births, listed means to prevent prematurity. Of the seven listed, two deal with public health measures. The most important of these was: "improve maternal nutrition—early in pregnancy and preferably before conception." (15)

A further element compounding the problem, and bearing directly on our argument, is the observation that the ultimate intellectual achievement of low birth weight infants is subnormal. This is a handicap our nation can ill afford.

TABLE 3

National rank and State	Per capita income, 1956	Infant mortality rate, 1963		Percent nonwhite births, 1960
		White	Nonwhite	
1 Connecticut	$3,678	21.0	41.0	5.4
2 Delaware	3,563	20.9	38.7	17.9
3 Illinois	3,511	20.3	41.2	15.4
50 Mississippi	1,751	22.9	57.6	54.9
49 South Carolina	2,027	22.4	48.1	43.0
45 Kentucky	2,205	26.3	44.4	8.7
44 North Carolina	2,235	22.2	50.8	32.6

Sources: National Statistical Abstract, U.S.A.; Infant, Fetal and Maternal Mortality, National Center for Health Statistics, series 20, No. 3, 1966.

Geographic areas with the lowest per capita income and the highest incidence of poverty have the highest infant mortality rates. In general, states with the highest per capita incomes have the lowest infant mortality and those at the bottom of the economic ladder the highest. Since these statewide data average affluent counties and poverty counties, they give only part of the picture of disparity between the rich and the poor. The impact of poverty can be best appreciated by examining the performance, county by county. The distribution of mortality rates by deciles isolates these data with unambiguous clarity. The percentage of counties with infant mortality rates 50 percent higher than the national average for white births is shockingly high among the impoverished and negligible among the rich states. Though clearly the impact of births in the nonwhite population is to raise the mortality figures, a state like Kentucky with a very low level of Negro births still has poverty counties with rates significantly higher than those found in affluent, predominantly white counties. Some of the rates found among our Negro citizens are worse than those existing in Africa, South America, and Asia. What is disheartening is that the gap between the white and the nonwhite groups is widening. . . .

. . . .

The cold statistics confirm that the existence of poverty has an adverse effect upon our national economic posture: Those living in poverty represent a continuing economic drain; the dole is inflationary; those reared in poverty cannot enter the employment market; and poverty is self-perpetuating. In regions of Appalachia and sections of our urban slums, a third generation of Americans is being reared in poverty. This is stated most strikingly in the following quotation from a report by Peter Schrag in which he reappraised Appalachia in 1968:

"Appalachia, now growing its third welfare generation, has counties where more than a third of the population is unemployed, where the government check—social security, welfare, aid to dependent children—is the prime source of income, and where some men are so far from their last job that it cannot properly be said that they have a trade at all. Here the average adult has a sixth-grade education, three-fourths of the children who start school drop out before they complete the 12th grade, and the statistics of human pathology—tuberculosis, silicosis, infant mortality—are so high that they do not belong in the Western world at all." . . .

. . . .

The feeding of our children is a pressing national emergency and all our current efforts hardly measure up to the challenge. What can be done to meet the need? . . .

. . . .

The food industries of the United States should take the initiative, enter into a unique partnership with government, at the federal, state, and local levels, and in conjunction with a philanthropic foundation, undertake responsible action to insure solution. Model nutrition programs can and must be established in well-circumscribed geographic areas where poverty is known to exist and the presence of malnutrition substantiated. All the resources of industry for supply, education, and distribution must be marshalled and an attempt made to lift the nutritional level of the area. Follow the guide lines established in overseas programs: reorient eating habits by nutrition education at all levels, encourage local participation and implementation and help to establish the necessary local agencies to perpetuate the programs once external sponsorship retires. The food industry can make programs work. It has the financial resources. In 1965 it was the second largest manufacturing group in the country, with a value of manufactured products in excess of $23 billion and a net income before taxes of over $14 billion. It has the technical knowledge of food production and distribution and its member concerns are masters of the art of salesmanship. As evidence we can cite their success in establishing products for nutrient supplementation in developing countries: "Vitasay" in Hong Kong, "Pronutro" in South America, and "Incapurina" in Latin America. The illustrations concern only food supplements, but the lesson learned can be applied to nutrition as a whole, and they indicate the critical role that the food industry can play in determining the success of such programs.

Utilize the local food store or supermarket not only as a distributive agency, but also as an educational arena; assure that within the selected geographic area the basic federal support programs are operative, particularly the Food Stamp and Commodities Distribution programs. Involve the schools, the churches, the civic organizations, and community action programs; educate, distribute, improvise, and feed. Demonstrate to the world that we have not only the food but the imagination to insure that none go hungry, and can do so not by demanding only more federal dollars, but rather by recruiting an imaginative and creative program spurred by private industry working with a foundation and government. To fail is to court disaster. Not to try is cowardly. To succeed is to open new vistas of national productivity.

The obligations of the private sector become clear in the following quotation: "Economic policy in the United States economy, which now enjoys a productive power and wealth outdistancing the most fanciful expectations of a decade ago, is ultimately a moral problem. The traditional economic problems have become secondary not because they are no longer of prime importance, but rather because they are relatively solved. We have learned conclusively how to avoid great depressions, and we have made significant progress toward reducing the frequency and scope of even minor recessions. But we are not facing up adequately to the ultimate moral question that underlies all economic endeavors: What portions of our total annual product should be devoted to the ultimate purposes of serving pressing social needs, lest wealth accumulate and men decay?"

The future of our country depends upon those with imagination, compassion, energy, and determination. They can, through exercise of these talents, lift our children from poverty by assuring that none will live in want of food.

Prepared Statement of Marvin Davies, Florida Field Director National Association for the Advancement of Colored People (NAACP), Before the United States Senate Select Committee on Nutrition and Human Needs, Bethune School, Immokalee, Collier County, Florida, March 10, 1969 at 1:00 O'Clock P.M.

Mr. Chairman and Committee Members: My name is Marvin Davies and I am the Florida Field Director for the National Association for the Advancement of Colored People (NAACP) whose national office is located at 1790 Broadway in New York City and Florida State Office at 1125 22nd Street South, St. Petersburg, Florida (Pinellas County).

The NAACP National Office has requested that I present the views of the NAACP with reference to hunger, malnutrition and the general condition of migratory and agricultural farm workers in the State of Florida.

For almost 61 years the working and living conditions of agricultural workers in the United States, especially of Negro farm workers, have been matters of great concern of the National Association for the Advancement of Colored People.

Prior to my appointment as Florida Field Director for the Association, I had been closely associated with the plight, frustration, concern and problems of the migratory agricultural workers in my native State of Florida.

As a Social Worker with the State Department of Public Welfare I have worked very closely with the seasonal agricultural farm workers. My case load consisted of a ridiculous high of 220 farm labor family clients. The welfare unit to which I was assigned was responsible for serving the area commonly known as the "muck" in Palm Beach County. My travel and work covered the areas and camps of Belle Glade, Pakokee Bean City, Canal Point, Lake Harbor, Chosen and South Bay. On special assignments I have had to work with clients in Moorehaven, Clewiston, and Labelle.

Also, prior to 1966 I was employed in Fort Myers, the City of my residence, as a teacher in the public school system. Rather than to hear my outcry of injustice to the Negroes of Lee County the School Board fired me. I was subsequently employed as a substitute teacher in both Charlotte and Collier counties. In fact, I taught for almost a year right here at the Bethune School in Immokalee. At this very school is where I really saw hunger and malnutrition at their worst. There were white lips on black children, a sure sign of hunger. I witnessed "pot bellies" which made constant sounds of distress, a sure sign of malnutrition.

I have seen children whose only verbal sound was heard at the command of the teacher to prepare for lunch. Too, I have witnessed the flow of tears at the same command because there was no money to purchase a school lunch. The only continuing sounds that were assured from these children were those of agony, pain and the cry of acids in the digestive tract. I have also seen brown paper bags opened during the lunch hour to reveal only a cold piece of corn bread, cold biscuit and a small container of molasses. Occasionally there will be a piece of cold pork, fat back or neck bones.

Not only have I witnessed these shocking and continuing realities, but I have found myself in the loading areas at 4:30 o'clock in the mornings; I have worked with clients and parents housed in the pathetic match-boxes and shacks; I have known babies to die from malnutrition; I have seen five and six year olds trying to prepare a meal for smaller brothers and sisters; I have had clients with no job, food or adequate clothing; I have witnessed clients earning less than child care expense after a 12 hour days work.

I have reached the conclusion, based upon my work and direct involvement, that the 100,000 seasonal agricultural workers in the State of Florida are the victims of the most extreme abuse and exploitation to be found anywhere in the United States. In fact, it is my opinion that farm labor conditions in this state constitute a serious national disgrace, if not a deliberate conspiracy involving the U.S. Congress, U.S. Government agencies, state, county and local business and public officials. . . .

TABLE 4. HOUSEHOLDS with POOR DIETS, by State: Spring 1965

State	Percent	Number
	(households in State = 100)	thousands
Northeast		
Connecticut	16	123
Maine	20	53
Massachusetts	17	258
New Hampshire	18	34
New Jersey	16	298
New York	17	906
Pennsylvania	18	576
Rhode Island	19	47
Vermont	20	21
North Central		
Illinois	21	629
Indiana	22	297
Iowa	24	187
Kansas	23	152
Michigan	21	466
Minnesota	23	219
Missouri	24	314
Nebraska	24	99
North Dakota	24	41

TABLE 4. HOUSEHOLDS with POOR DIETS, by State: Spring 1965 (Cont.)

State	Percent	Number
	(households in State = 100)	thousands
Ohio	21	592
South Dakota	25	46
Wisconsin	22	241
South		
Alabama	25	227
Arkansas	27	143
Delaware	21	27
District of Columbia	23	55
Florida	24	416
Georgia	25	279
Kentucky	25	211
Louisiana	25	227
Maryland	20	186
Mississippi	27	155
North Carolina	25	314
Oklahoma	24	179
South Carolina	26	159
Tennessee	25	259
Texas	24	684
Virginia	24	265
West Virginia	24	116
West		
Arizona	18	73
California	16	860
Colorado	18	95
Idaho	18	34
Montana	18	35
Nevada	16	20
New Mexico	18	44
Oregon	17	96
Utah	17	42
Washington	17	143
Wyoming	17	15

Source: Estimated from patterns of dietary adequacy determined from ARS 62-17 in conjunction with counts of households from Census reports, 1960 and 1965. U.S.D.A.

Chapter Three

HEALTH

Whether or not millions of our citizens receive adequate medical care is no longer a question to be asked—they do not. The cost of medical care has escalated to the point where even middle-income families can not afford to get sick.

The health problems faced by our poor are of an even greater magnitude. They are forced to live under the most unsanitary conditions, exposing themselves to serious diseases. They do not have the financial ability to pay, at least in full, and therefore find themselves forced to depend upon public medical assistance of one kind or another. They find that doctors are in scare supply in their areas, and, once they arrive at the clinic, their ills and complaints are frequently handled in an uncivilized and demeaning manner. Travelling from residence to clinic is usually time—consuming and costly. Often, they must make several trips since different types of services, such as pre—natal clinics, well—baby clinics, and innoculations, are scheduled on different days.

There is no longer any acceptable excuse in our society for slum Blacks having seven years less life—span that the average white.

Nor is there any excuse for the Negro infant mortality rate being three times that of the white or why four times as many Negro women die in childbirth as do whites.

The report of the American Health Association documents inadequate and inhumane medical care existing across our land. After visiting many areas of the United States the President and the President-elect of the Association concluded that it is time for health officials to witness first hand the sight and smell that is a part of the lives of millions of Americans, rather than restricting themselves to clinics, laboratories, and cold medical statistics. It is time that the medical profession demonstrate that it truly cares and start to lead the way out of this morass. It is time that the public understand these conditions in order to force the necessary improvements to be made. The present inadequacies are intolerable in any society, particularly in our nation, which we generally consider to be the wealthiest and most advanced on earth.

If You're Black and Sick*

Newsweek

"I went there at 9 o'clock like they said," recalled the young New York Negro mother. "About 12:30, I saw the doctor and he said I was in the wrong clinic. I went to the other clinic and waited until 2 o'clock and there were still people in front of me. The kids get out of school at 2:30, so I had to leave. That's just the way it is if you're poor."

To obtain a pre-natal physical, a polio shot, or a prescription for iron tablets, the resident of the inner city routinely faces such Kafkaesque encounters with crowded clinics, officious clerks and indifferent—or even contemptuous—doctors. And few of the 200 physicians, sociologists and public-health experts who met

---

* *Newsweek* (July 7, 1969),
   Copyright Newsweek, Inc., July 7, 1969.

last week at Wentworth–by–the–Sea in Portsmouth, N.H., to discuss medicine in the ghettos, could improve upon the young woman's summation of the problem.

And even the incongruously lush surroundings of the New Hampshire seaside resort failed to obscure the harsh facts about the inadequacy of health care for the inner city poor, nor conceal the bitterness of some of the Negro spokesmen. In matters of health, noted Richard Hatcher, the black mayor of Gary, Indiana, Negroes are "the victims of an unresponsive medical community within an unresponsive social framework." To underline the results of white indifference, the experts considered again the litany of by–now familiar statistics: the slum Negro has a life expectancy that is seven years shorter than the average U.S. white. Infant mortality is three times higher for Negroes than it is for whites, and in most cities, four times as many Negro women die in childbirth than do white women. Among the babies who do survive, thousands suffer from mental retardation because their mothers were malnourished and obtained inadequate prenatal care.

Shortage: Clearly, a major reason for the poor state of health in the ghetto is a shortage of physicians. The same discrimination that has kept most Negroes in the slums, Hatcher noted, has kept them out of medical schools. With Negroes comprising more than 10 per cent of the U.S. population, only 2 per cent of American doctors are black. And in the ghetto, there are few doctors either black or white. Drs. Alfred Haynes and Michael R. McGarvey cited surveys showing that in Chicago there were 62 doctors for every 100,000 residents of poverty areas, compared with 126 per 100,000 in more prosperous sections of the city. And in the shadow of Baltimore's Johns Hopkins Hospital, they reported, there is only one doctor for every 6,600 residents— a ratio "lower than that of some of the so–called developing countries." Moreover, the biggest shortage of physicians occurs among the specialists who are most needed in the ghetto— obstetricians, pediatricians and internists.

Not surprisingly, in view of the scarcity of doctors, the slum resident's family doctor is often whoever happens to be on duty in the hospital emergency room. Many of the residents of Watts take a two-hour bus trip to get care at Los Angeles County General Hospital. On an average day, some 1,200 patients appear in the admitting-examining room at Chicago's Cook County Hospital. Whether they receive the kind of sympathetic attention most Americans require of a family physician is questionable. Many hospitals reject patients who aren't "interesting clinical material," Haynes and McGarvey note. And slum dwellers themselves wryly refer to municipal hospital clinics as "the butchershop" or "the plantation."

Belatedly, to be sure, the white community has begun to do something about the crowded outpatient waiting rooms and the long trips to emergency clinics. Since 1965, the U.S. Office of Economic Opportunity has spent some $146 million to establish 41 health centers designed to give comprehensive care within ghetto neighborhoods. Chicago's Mile-Square Health Center, operating in a three-story converted apartment building, serves some 30,000 residents of the West Side. Affiliated with Presbyterian-St. Luke's Hospital, the center provides a complete program of preventive medicine—including dental care, prenatal consultation and pediatric services.

To help bring the center's services to the neighborhood, the center employs some 30 community health aides recruited from within the ghetto and given a ten-week course in such matters as home nursing, nutrition and sanitation. They are also qualified to advise ghetto residents on how to reach responsible authorities with complaints about poor garbage collection or infractions of housing codes. "You can't separate the medical problems from the social problems," a center spokesman points out.

Control: Such centers pose the same issue of community control that has caused strife in city schools. Mile-Square works with an advisory committee of 30 neighborhood residents who range from professional men to welfare recipients. The committee must approve the hiring of all the center's non-professional personnel, and a committee member interviews doctors and nurses and other professionals who are candidates for jobs at the center.

But the deep distrust of the Negro community toward the hospitals, medical schools and doctors of the white establishment has already surfaced in battles over community control. A health center on Chicago's West Side was burned during the 1966 riots. Even in a new location like the Martin Luther King Jr. Family Health Center, troubles continue. The neighborhood advisory council accused the all-white trustees of Mount Sinai Hospital, with which the center is affiliated, of failing to consult on the hiring of employees, and of placing an unfair ceiling on salaries of center workers.

After a three-day strike last April, the ties to Mount Sinai were severed and the center's white director was fired. "The community and the center are having grass-roots problems," admits the new director, Dr. Kermit T. Mehlinger (a black). "There are a lot of areas of conflict since there are many community organizations and some of these are not democratically organized."

The question of who is going to run medical programs for the ghetto poor, it became clear at the meeting, isn't going to be solved easily. The medical needs of blacks, some speakers suggested, are so distinctly different from those of whites that a black separatism in health care may be the only answer. Perhaps, suggested Dr. Nathan Hare, chairman of the Black Studies Institute at San Francisco State College, the U.S. Negro will have to create a Black Public Health Service, a Black Association for Mental Health and even a Black Cross to assure improved health care for Negroes.

No Future: Most of the experts agreed that medical care in the inner city should be administered by the community. But first, noted Dr. Leonard Cronkhite of Children's Hospital Medical Center in Boston, must come an adequate supply of competent professionals—including doctors—from the ghetto. The best answer, of course, would come from a sweeping change in the social structure of the cities which would eliminate ghettos.

"I hope," said Dr. John C. Holloman of New York, "that there is no future for the ghetto physician, and no future for the ghetto."

Health Crisis In America*

A Report by the American Public Health Association

Introduction

In the summer of 1969, as President and President-elect of the American Public Health Association, we undertook a tour to examine in microcosm health conditions in the United States.

The tour started in a Mexican-American barrio in Houston. From there, we went to a rural community in the Central Valley of California; juvenile and adult detention quarters in Atlanta, Georgia; the Potomac River in Washington, D.C.; homes of off-reservation Indians in Great Falls, Montana; and the inner-city community of Kenwood-Oakland on the Southside of Chicago, Illinois. Our aim was to investigate, firsthand, typical environmental and medical care situations which give rise to serious health problems in our country. We believed it was time for health professionals to see directly, to hear and smell these situations which characterize the lives of millions of Americans, rather than to limit our view of the problems to health statistics, patients in clinics and laboratory specimens.

Acknowledgment

This work was supported in part by participation of staff of the Citizens Board of Inquiry Into Health Services For Americans and by a grant for publication from the Field Foundation, for all of which deep appreciation is expressed.

People from the neighborhoods, concerned professionals, some

* U.S. Senate Select Committee on Nutrition and Human Needs, November 1969.

health and welfare officials, national and state legislators, and representatives of the news media joined our tour. . . .

. . . .

Approximately 50,000 persons of the Kenwood-Oakland area of Chicago, who live in rodent- and insect-infested housing, with broken plumbing, stairs and windows. Today, these people pay from one- to two-thirds of their income for rent and are served by a total of five physicians in their community—a physician-to-population ratio less than one-tenth of the country as a whole—with the county hospital and clinics eight miles away.

A 53-year-old American Indian in Great Falls, Montana, veteran of the South Pacific in World War II, raising a family of six children (and one grandchild, whose father is now in Vietnam) on a pension and what he can scrounge by salvage in a junkyard. He can neither afford to buy food stamps nor return to the hospital for post-cancer treatment—closure of his bowel, which now opens on his abdomen—because his family would not have food while he is gone.

The farmworker in Tulare County, California, who said that exposure to pesticides from airplane spraying of fields, contrary to regulations and often leading to illness, was frequently not reported because "What's the use?" she asked. "We lose wages going to the doctor, get better in a week usually, and get no compensation, and they don't stop spraying."

The woman in Tulare County, eight months pregnant, whose Medi-Cal (Medicaid) eligibility had been cancelled last month because her husband had just found a temporary job, thus forcing her to seek care at the County Hospital which previous experience had taught her to hate.

The young woman in Houston, whose welfare check for a family of eight had been cut from $123 to $23 a month.

A therapist in the Child Treatment Center, Atlanta, Georgia, where excellent work with youngsters in trouble was underway, but "the main difficulty is that the kids have to go right back to the same life that got them into trouble in the first place, and we can't do anything about that here."

The "uncooperative" chronic alcoholic who carried a card from Atlanta's Grady Hospital identifying him as an epileptic, but who, a few days before our visit, had occupied the "hole"— a 4 feet by 8 feet solitary confinement cell in the Atlanta City Prison.

Dead fish floating in the dirty water of the Potomac, the "Nation's River," which flows through our capital city so polluted by untreated and inadequately treated sewage that fish cannot live there, and the spread of human disease-causing bacteria appears as a serious threat.

Everywhere we encountered lamentable excuses offered by local health and welfare officials, who seemed as trapped by "the rules" as the people they were supposed to serve.

While there has been considerable improvement in the quality of life for most Americans, the fact still remains that a large proportion of the 20,000,000 Blacks, the 5,000,000 Mexican-Americans, the 500,000 American Indians, and millions of others live day in and day out in conditions we would not let our animals endure; and the "system" of care for people with disease associated with such conditions seems mainly to obstruct their receiving the care that is needed. . . .

A Mexican-American Barrio, Houston, Texas

"The average Mexican-American lives ten years less than the average Anglo. There is no biological reason why this should be so. The only reason is because the Mexican-American is starving and does not have enough medical care"—Senator Ralph Yarborough, D-Texas.

In Houston—the space-age city with world renowned heart transplant facilities as well as astronauts and the Astrodome— we visited a community of 80,000 Mexican-Americans who live in the center of the city.

We walked through the Canales Courts area in the western portion of the Second Ward and visited the homes of residents there. In this five-square-block area, approximately 2,000 Mexican-Americans live in 432 apartments. Rents average between $40 and $60 a month, not including utilities. Neighborhood people informed us that the day before our visit the city had paved their street and made one of its infrequent attempts to pick up the garbage and cut the weeds. The Canales Courts area is typical of the neighborhood in which most of Houston's 80,000 Mexican-Americans live.

The first person with whom we spoke was a 50-year-old Mexican-American grandmother. She lives with her mother and 2-year-old grandson, left by a daughter who was unable to care for him. The building containing their tiny two-room apartment once might have comfortably housed a single family but now has been divided into eight cramped apartments in which eight families, 40 people, live. The two rooms of her apartment were about ten feet by 12 feet. . . .

.   .   .   .

Seeing us look at the plaster dust which was sifting through her ceiling into the pots on her stove, and at her grandson who was sleeping on what served as a bed while flies and mosquitoes rested on his face, she said, "It's such a struggle to just keep things where they are without them getting any worse."

This stooped, grey-haired woman had watched four of her twelve children die from diarrhea, a common disease in children who suffer from malnutrition. Her hand was in a clumsy bandage she had fixed to protect a burn wound suffered over a month ago. The burn had never been treated by a doctor, and its effects may have been aggravated by the diabetes from which she suffered. The diabetes requires continuing medical attention, but "sometimes it is just impossible for me to get to the hospital for medicine since I can't even pay for the bus."

When she does have busfare, the visit to the hospital for the necessary treatment is likely to take most of the day. The only bus routes which serve the Second Ward run to and from the downtown area. To travel by bus from the Canales Courts area to Ben Taub County Hospital at the Texas Medical Center, she has to catch an eastbound bus for a 15 minute, 2 mile ride to downtown and then transfer to a southbound bus for a 25 minute, 6 mile ride. She may wait at each bus stop for as long as a half hour. Thus, every time she leaves to visit the hospital, she faces the possibility of an hour and 40 minute trip each way, in addition to the usually long wait for treatment at the hospital itself.

For the people of the Canales Courts area, Ben Taub Hospital is the closest of the two county hospitals which serve welfare recipients. Since there are almost no bilingual personnel on the hospital staff, Mexican-American patients often receive reproachful lectures about their inability to speak English. "Our children get sicker than most," one lady told us, "but they don't like to go to the doctor, because nobody speaks Spanish." . . .

. . . .

Despite the near 100-degree heat, residents of the Second Ward came out of their homes to tell about mosquitoes "which eat you alive" and rats that are " 'this big' and scare away the cats." Mrs. H. said her 2½-year-old neighbor had been bitten two days before by a copperhead snake in her own yard and it took 45 minutes to drive the child to the county hospital. Another resident told how he kept his children inside his home because of rats and snakes. Some children must stay outside while their parents are at work. They may go to a park which was described by one young man as "a place where we have to play all day with the rats and mosquitoes and we don't even have any trees or shade."

Several residents described problems with rats. "There are rats even in the rectory here, but the church can pay for cheese and traps," Father Emile Farge reported. "Many of my neighbors cannot afford even traps." Dr. Charles A. Pigford, City Health Department Director, responded that the city has a rat control program, but not sufficient funds to conduct an adequate program. . . .

. . . .

Another problem of the young in Canales Courts is gross tooth decay. "A great number of Mexican-Americans lose their teeth at an early age," said Dr. Mervin Mergele, Director of Houston's Dental Health Division. "Dental care is too expensive for most of these people and they can't afford the foods which help build good teeth." Ripley House, a private settlement home in the

Mexican-American neighborhood, conducts a small-scale dental program for children. Ben Taub Hospital, one of two sources of care for welfare residents, has only an oral surgery program for adults. "Although a few extractions take place here, much more could be done than just taking out teeth," Dr. Mergele asserted. . . .

Tulare County, San Joaquin Valley, California

"The poor child in a rural community may grow up hungry while surrounded by food he cannot eat. He leaves school too soon because his labor is needed to support his family. He lives in crowded, broken down housing, and is denied educational, medical, and recreational services that are taken for granted among the urban poor. Rural America needs her young people, yet we are wasting a generation by driving them into the urban ghettos." — Assemblyman Gordon W. Duffy, R-California.

Hidden behind the peaceful green of the San Joaquin Valley with its productive farmlands and plentiful fruit groves lives thousands of farm families — in another world, of poverty and poor health.

Many of the Anglos whose fathers came from Oklahoma to find work in Tulare County a generation ago are foremen in the fields. The laborers are mainly Chicanos who came from Mexico to follow the crops and are now gradually forming more or less settled communities.

The use of pesticides in the fields is one of the most worrisome health problems of the workers. "When they use the pesticides, they spray us too," a worker said. "Sure we get sprayed, and we get sick. Sometimes you see people going around with headaches all the time and getting dizzy and they wonder what the matter is. It's the pesticides, the spray."

State regulations require that no airplane spraying be done while workers in the fields may be exposed, and that after spraying, signs be posted to keep workers out. But one worker told us: "We get red eyes many times from the sulphur the planes spray. The planes cover your clothes with sulphur and when you get home your kids hug you and they get sick too. Twice I was thinning peaches and picking oranges and the plane came over, spraying. We never knew it was coming. I took the number of the plane and told the foreman. Nothing happened."

An official from the County Agriculture Commission gave this response. "If there are violations, all people have to do is give us a call." When pressed as to how many prosecutions there had been for violations, he replied; "We've placed a number of operators on a year's probation, but you must remember that it's a very hard thing to take away a man's livelihood by taking his spray permit."

But what about the livelihood of workers who get sick in the fields? The official conceded however, that his inspectors have little time for anything beyond checking spray rigs and investigating a few complaints. Dr. Erwin Brauner of the Tulare County Medical Society disclosed that between 100 and 200 Tulare workers are reported to suffer from pesticide poisoning each year. Workers claim most cases are never reported. "What's the use?" one laborer asked. "We lose wages going to the doctor, get better in a week usually and get no compensation, and they don't stop the spraying." . . .

. . . .

"With no Medi-Cal card, I have to go to the county hospital. I feel so terrible to go there and say I cannot pay. I feel so ashamed." The county hospital does not require poor patients to pay in advance, but if a patient cannot pay the bill when it comes due, his property will be attached. The last time she traveled the 20 miles to the county hospital, she left at 7 a.m. because she had a morning appointment. "I didn't get home until one o'clock the next morning. We waited and waited." . . .

. . . .

When the family is not on welfare, however, they cannot use their Medi-Cal card. "Without our card, we can't afford to go to any doctor." During emergencies, she said it was difficult to get care because the county hospital was 30 miles away and was understaffed. . . .

A Child Treatment Center, and the "Stockade" Atlanta, Georgia

The Child Treatment Center

"These children have committed no crime except to have no home," an official of the Child Treatment Center said of the children in the area of the Center which is reserved for neglected or abandoned children. Also in the Center are detention facilities for boys and girls charged with delinquency of all degrees of severity, ranging from violation of the curfew ordinance to murder-manslaughter.

"These children all have one thing in common," a staff member remarked. "Their lives are filled with people who don't care, or with people who care but who cannot do anything to improve the situation." ...

. . . .

In the girl's section for delinquents, an 11-year-old pregnant girl was locked in with others who were there for a variety of offenses. Pregnant girls traditionally drop out of Atlanta schools. "So they often end up here," an official reported. ...

Care for alcoholics

"Alcoholism is the third major public health problem in the United States today. It is an extremely serious illness, involving some six million people in the United States. Contrary to public opinion, only 15 percent are 'skid row bums'. The remaining 85 per cent are 'nice people' — garden variety citizens — typically a 40-year-old white collar worker with a wife and children and a member of a church." Vernelle Fox, M.D., Medical Director, The Georgian Clinic.

"Every Monday morning we have a crowd and it's usually the same bunch," was the opening statement by an officer in the Fulton County Jail in Atlanta, Georgia.

Individuals accused of drunkenness are delivered to the jail's back door. After being admitted, they are searched. All valuables (such as glasses) are taken, marked, and returned upon departure. After being fingerprinted, the prisoners are taken to the jail where, on bare floor without beds or chairs, for the next four to eight hours, they "dry out."

When the prisoner is reasonably sober, he gets an opportunity to put up $25 bail. If he cannot pay or obtain the $25 immediately, he is held until the next session of the General Division of the Municipal Court, known as "drunk court." Lower class prisoners usually cannot pay and hence must appear in court for having been drunk. . . .

. . . .

State Representative Julian Bond who accompanied us on the tour remarked, "Whites are charged with the minor crimes and sent to the city jail, whereas Blacks are charged with major crimes and sent to the county jail."

On the day of the tour, 18 prisoners appeared in "drunk court." Any who agreed to participate in a private rehabilitation program were sent there for 30 days. Of the 18 offenders, six men and one woman volunteered to accept this program. The remaining group, ranging from a shriveled, old and obviously ill man to a healthy looking teenager, were sentenced to 13 days at the City Prison farm, locally called the "Stockade."

At the time of our visit to the Stockade, 363 men and 32 women were in the facility which has room for 600 people. "Our load is seasonal," the superintendent reported. "Right now, people have more work and so we have fewer prisoners."

When a prisoner arrives at the Stockade, he receives a blue and white uniform. All personal belongings of any value are taken for safekeeping until his departure. He then finds an empty bed in one of the wards, approximately 300 feet by 36 feet, two wards for male prisoners and one for female prisoners. There is no locker for the prisoner, not even a spot for a toothbrush. If he wants to read, he can carry a book into his ward, but the only place to keep it is under his mattress.

Each prisoner is assigned to work detail. "Work is therapy," explained the superintendent. A prisoner receives $1 for each day of work, the major type being farm work. When the superintendent was asked what he would like most to improve the Stockade, he answered, "A bigger farm."

If a prisoner thinks he should see a doctor, he can ask for the prison physician who spends about 45 minutes a day at the Stockade and during this time sees an average of 13 prisoners. Prisoners can receive more care if the doctor decides they should go to sick bay where typically two to five patients are kept, except during the winter when many patients are admitted with "flu." Two practical nurses are in charge of the sick bay. . . .

. . . .

One Stockade prisoner with a card from Grady Hospital certifying he was an epileptic said he had been arrested during an epileptic attack in front of the hospital where he was seeking care. In the Stockade, he had been placed in the "hole" for being uncooperative. He acknowledged that he had been in the Stockade several times previously for intoxication.

After seeing the Stockade, we had an opportunity to talk with Dr. Bernard Holland of Emory University. He described a highly successful pilot program for 1,200 "hard-core" alcoholics, but the program had ended July 1, 1969, when the Federal funds supporting it expired and local or state money could not be raised to continue it. An excellent staff was now being dispersed from this major effort in a University-directed program to treat alcoholism as a disease. . . .

. . . .

Potomac. The Nation's River Washington, D.C.

Dead fish, floating sewage, and rotting plant-life constitute much of the Potomac River flowing through the Nation's Capital. Down the river, a large sign warns, "Polluted Water, Bathing Hazardous." According to marine scientist Dr. Donald Lear, this means, "Anyone who comes in contact with this water should see a doctor."

Our visit to the Potomac was highlighted by a laboratory demonstration of the nature and extent of pollution in the river, prepared by the Federal Water Pollution Control Administration. Chemical, physical and biological tests of specimens of water from various places in the river show the severe degradation of the water.

The major contribution to the Potomac River's pollution comes from untreated domestic sewage. More than 400 million gallons of partially treated and raw sewage, mostly from homes in the Metropolitan Washington area, flow into the river each day. "Unlike other rivers of the country which are polluted by industrial wastes, this river's problem is people," Dr. Lear said. "We just have too many people for the treatment plants we have."
. . .

. . . .

In addition to the reduction of dissolved oxygen in the water of the Potomac which makes fish life in many parts of the river impossible, a new problem of even greater urgency has recently come to light. The water carries a high bacterial count and Salmonella have been isolated throughout 15 to 20 miles of the river. The latter type organism causes human disease, usually in the form of food-poisoning, and some varieties can be fatal. Other agents of human disease, including the virus causing hepatitis, may be present in sewage-contaminated water.

More than 42,000 acres of shellfish grounds in the river already have been closed by health authorities. These authorities fear human disease may occur from eating shellfish grown in waters with gross sewage contamination.

Also, fish may become infected with disease-causing organisms in the polluted Potomac and then swim to clean waters. When caught, these infected fish may cause disease to unsuspecting people.

Indians Who Leave the Reservation, Great Falls, Mont.

. . . "While significant improvements have been made in the health status of reservation Indians served by the Indian Health Service since 1955, it is recognized that many Indians living in urban and non-reservation communities have not fully shared in these advances. Constraints of Federal policy and the limitation of resources do not permit the service to provide them with the comprehensive health services which are available to Indians on reservations" — Emery A. Johnson, M.D., Acting Director, Indian Health Service.

The Indian who has left the reservation is in many ways a forgotten man. He has cast aside the dependent status of a reservation Indian to make his way in a world for which he is basically unprepared. Yet in making the transition, he can expect little, if any, help from the very institutional system which preordained his lack of preparation. Federal programs designed to serve reservation Indians can no longer meet his needs. State and local health and welfare programs, ill-conceived to meet the general needs of the poor, are utterly unequipped to deal with the special problems arising from the Indian's prior dependent status and from his culture and language. Caught in this institutional gap, he may if he is lucky come to eke out a marginal existence off the reservation, but more likely he will return to the reservation where at least he can get the bare necessities of life.
. . .

During this initial period off the reservation, an Indian's health care needs are supposed to be met by the Indian Health Service (IHS). Indians who have left the reservation ordinarily remain eligible to receive care at IHS facilities. But because the IHS was established primarily to serve reservation Indians, almost all of its facilities are located on reservations. From Great Falls, the nearest reservation is Rocky Boys, which is well over 100 miles away. To expect people to travel over 100 miles in a nonemergency situation is unrealistic. To ask people to travel that far in an emergency situation is inhumane. For many the trip is still longer. One young mother told us of taking her child to her home reservation, Fort Belknap, for extensive medical attention, since there would have been no place for her to stay at Rocky Boys while the child was convalescing. Besides, she said, friends and relatives at the reservation could take her in. Fort Belknap is nearly 200 miles from Great Falls; if she had been from Fort Peck or Northern Cheyenne, she would have had to travel 350 or 400 miles before her child could receive care.

For an Indian in his first year off the reservation, the IHS has made some attempt to mitigate the harshness of this situation. It has established a policy of reimbursing local hospitals or doctors for emergency care given an Indian who is less than one year off the reservation. But the relief provided by this policy is largely illusory. According to Emery A. Johnson, M.D., Acting Director of IHS, constraints of Federal policy and the limitation of resources do not permit the Service to provide them with the comprehensive health services which are available to Indians on reservations. . . .

. . . .

Thus, if an Indian, newly arrived in Great Falls, receives treatment from a local doctor, he may well discover that he is stuck with a bill the IHS refuses to pay. Under these circumstances, many Indians choose not to risk responsibility for a large medical bill and simply do not seek help. In an emergency, others may discover the IHS will not cover their expenses and, as a result, suffer the humiliation and inconvenience of having to leave the local facility and make the long trip to an IHS facility. We met an Indian girl who told of being turned away from the county hospital when she was ready to have her baby. Presumably, the hospital learned the IHS would not cover the costs of the delivery. "They told me that I didn't qualify for welfare and should go back to my reservation." Her baby was born over 100 miles away at the Rocky Boys Reservation. . . .

. . . .

One of the residents of Wire Mill Road is a 53-year-old World War II veteran of the South Pacific. He receives a monthly veterans' disability pension, which covers only his rent and utilities. His utilities include a pit privy situated 50 feet from the house near an enclosed cistern which contains the entire water supply for a month. The cistern pump was defective when we were there. For the 500 gallons of water delivered each month, approximately the amount used in one day by the average family of four, he pays $3. A waterline runs under the hill, but is controlled by the neighboring industrial complex. Residents of Wire Mill Road are not permitted to use it.

In the winter, it is nearly impossible for him to remove the garbage because the road to his home is not graveled. On the day of our visit, in the middle of summer, no garbage had been removed for a week because his only truck needed repair.

He does not qualify for general assistance because of his veterans' pension. Nine years ago, he had a colostomy for cancer of the bowel. He has never returned for the second operation, to close the colostomy, because he cannot afford the time away from work. Work for this World War II veteran is salvaging auto parts from the junkyard on the side of the hill. On a good day, he earns about two dollars. "If I can find junk to sell, then I can feed my family. If I can't find any...."

Feeding the family has become more expensive since the wood-burning oven broke down and it became necessary to purchase bread. His family includes a wife, six children — one of whom is partially blind — and one grandchild whose father is in Vietnam. Food stamps are an impossible dream; he cannot afford the lump sum payment of $36, the monthly amount required to purchase stamps for a family his size.

We asked his most pressing health problem. "A job," he replied.

Today, the hill, liberally strewn with junk from the city, is called "Hill 57" in recognition, legend has it, of the wealth of empty "Heinz 57" cans that once could be found scattered on the grounds. Across town from Wire Mill Road, Hill 57 is inhabited by a small, determined band of 15 Indian families, proud of their heritage and culture and unwilling to lose their identity by complete assimiliation into the white man's world. They live in small dilapidated shacks, seven or eight members to a family. Most of the Hill's residents are children. Until two years ago, these children suffered serious, recurring bouts of diarrhea; they had no running water. Now there is one faucet to serve all the families.
. . .

Chapter Four

Education

Ask a typical class of students, "What is the solution to the problems confronting America?" and the answer will almost certainly follow: "Education." This panacea for the world's ills can often be just the reverse—it may well be the means by which a person stays in the same state of deprivation into which he was born.

Studies have been made showing that today's public schools operate not as vehicles for social mobility but, rather as devices for securing and maintaining the status quo. Of course no one would admit to this dilemma. To be against advancement is un-American. Rather the approach most often used to insure permanent second-class status is the argument of maintaining neighborhood schools. How can anyone argue with that?

We can argue with it and we must. The time has long since passed for this kind of foolish debate. Equal educational opportunity must mean just that. We must see to it that all children have the necessary materials, good competent teachers, and adequate facilities. If we fail to provide substantial and meaningful educational opportunity for all, the prediction made by the Kerner Commission of two societies in America—one poor, one rich; one black, one white; one educated and one ignorant—may become a frightening reality.

A Portrait of Blight*

Muriel Crosby

The Disadvantaged

Teachers who have worked over a period of years with large numbers of disadvantaged children have little difficulty in identifying them. These teachers readily recognize characteristics which, if not treated and redirected, foretell failure for the school in making education count in the lives of children and their families.

What does a teacher see when he looks at his disadvantaged children?

A Self-Image That Reflects Worthlessness

Thousands of boys and girls entering the elementary school as five and six year olds have already learned that they are worth little. Life has taught them this in a short span of time. Many do not know who their parents are; they have been shunted around among other adults, living in many homes. Many have a one-parent home, often living with their mothers and brothers and sisters in a fatherless home. Children in the same family group sometimes have a number of different fathers. These youngsters are accustomed to seeing a succession of men in the home whose relations with the mother are transitory. *Such*

---

* *Educational Leadership*, 20 (February, 1963). Copyright by the Association for Supervision and Curriculum Development, 1963. Reprinted with permission.

children lack the stability of normal family life centered in the welfare of the children which helps a child feel important and wanted.

Poverty That Overwhelms

Disadvantaged children are basically economically deprived. Many of these children have never known what it means to go to sleep for the night with full stomachs. Their only complete meal each day is obtained as "free lunch" at school. One child who was having her first lunch at school was observed carefully wrapping half of her sandwich. On being questioned, she explained that her father was hungry; there had been no food in the house for three days.

Economically deprived children suffer because of poor and inadequate housing. Let the children describe how they live:

Franklin: "My family would like to move to another house because when it is cold the owner will not give us much heat to keep us warm. My mother said she was going to move when she finds a good house. That's what would please us the best."

Earl: "I wish we had enough food, money, and clothes for every one in our house. Sometimes we run out of food and money, and when we run out of money the bills pile up."

Ursula: "The best thing that could happen to my family is to move. I would like to move from the place we are living because of the living conditions. It is very bad. It is also a very slum area. We have no backyard to play in nor front. My sisters and brothers don't go outside unless we take them. So I think that is the best thing that could happen to my family."

Samuel: "If we had more money we could get a house over Riverside because the apartment is falling apart. The door is falling down. The ceiling is falling down and when it rains the rain comes in. We have roaches now but I hope we won't have them if we move over to Riverside."

Louis: "I wish that we could have a new house because the old house leaks when it snows. It has no backyard to play in and we will meet new friends."

Jacob: "I would want my family to have an icebox so that

every time my mother puts some meat in it it would not spoil, and so that we won't have to throw anything away and go to the store to buy more food to put in it again."

Among the deprived, physical survival blots out all other needs. In many families, mother is the sole breadwinner. With long work hours in unskilled employment, the mother is away from home during most of the child's waking hours. The demands upon the mother during her short time at home make it impossible for her to meet the needs of growing children. Family meals are unknown in many instances.

The oldest children in the family are forced to assume the burdens of maturity too early in life. They handle the family food budget, shopping while mother is at work. They prepare whatever food is available for younger children. They often assume full responsibility for youngers brothers and sisters. One nine year old explained that he loved his neighbor because she took care of his little brothers and sisters so that he could play.

Among the economically deprived are many whose health has been crippled. Poor nutrition, insufficient food, inadequate clothing and housing, and lack of simple, routine medical care have made deep inroads prior to school entrance. In one typical city, 65 percent of all public school children have never known what it means to have a family doctor, nor any medical service, except emergency clinic care. A preventive program of inoculations, vaccinations, annual physical examinations, and dental service must be provided by the school.

Many disadvantaged children are the victims of a poverty so crushing that early in life poor health not only drains the energy, but blights the spirit.

Values That Block Personal Development
and Social Development

For many disadvantaged children moral and spiritual perversion is the price of deprivation. Cramped and crowded living space, denying any form of privacy, early sensitizes the child to adult sexual behavior before he is mature enough to comprehend the significance of it. He is often the victims of adults living in his home. This is particularly true of girls who often become mothers when they are little more than children. Illegitimacy is an accepted pattern of life, and marriage of little consequence in sexual relationships.

The source of family income frequently affects the values developed by the disadvantaged child. Many children are growing up in an environment in which, for several generations, the chief source of income is from public and private welfare agencies. A pattern is established wherein it is normal and acceptable to receive financial support without individual effort and initiative. This factor, together with an early awareness of the fact that, to many, racial discrimination closes the door to opportunities for work, results in attitudes of defeatism and acceptance of the status quo. It produces generations of children without hope and the will to become individuals with a sense of dignity and worth.

A value system bred in deprivation is in sharp conflict with the established "middle-class" value system held by the school and community. And we find youngsters caught in the bind, rejected but not knowing why.

Blocks to Education

The disadvantaged child suffers most when he comes to school. His experience in living has ill prepared him for the demands of the typical school. Shaped by an environment whose harshness has indelibly stamped him in his own eyes as a person of little worth, he now must be able to conform in a situation which places primary emphasis upon verbal skills. He finds that his natural vocabulary fails to communicate; and the school's means of communication, informal standard English, is almost a second language to him. He resolves this problem often by becoming quiet, and his teacher classifies him as lacking in language facility and unable to express himself, in spite of the fact that his natural language is often dynamic and that he is quite facile in its use.

Next, the disadvantaged child becomes the victim of the group intelligence test. Lacking the experiences and the language tools which are incorporated in the typical group intelligence test, the child emerges from this measurement of experiences he has never known as a "slow learner," one whose potential is severely limited. And his teacher proceeds to build his curriculum upon a false diagnosis, thereby making certain that a low ceiling for potential is permanently established. In many schools, the matter is confounded by rigid segregation based on the findings of group intelligence and achievement tests, thereby blocking the deprived child from the stimulation of association with more fortunate children.

And, finally, the typical school holds onto common standards and common curriculum, sometimes watered down for the deprived. *The disadvantaged child early discovers that there is little relationship between the problems in living and his living in school.* He early discovers that there is little "use value" in what he learns in school and he leaves it behind him when he leaves the school each evening. This is the child for whom, figuratively, "drop-out" is the first entry on his school registration card the day he enters kindergarten.

Which Road

The situation of the disadvantaged child, the one for whom "failure" succinctly describes the school's prognosis, is not totally dismal. Increasing numbers of the disadvantaged, frequently found in urban areas, but not exclusively so, are finding hope in their schools.

The tremendous acceleration of change, chiefly characterized by social forces of mobility, racial desegregation, industrial mechanization, and world political tensions, is finding a parallel in changing concepts of education. Never before have educators been confronted with such difficult choices in selecting the road we will take and the directions we will follow.

Part of the difficulty is centered in the *bind* in which we find ourselves—wherein man's vastly accelerating conquest of the universe has left far behind his achievements in the social and spiritual aspects of his world. We find man standing at the crossroads. Here his choice may be, on the one hand, a broad, dual highway in which the achievements of his intellectual might are enmeshed with the needs of his spirit, each supporting and lending strength in reaching his ultimate destination: a world in which men live in harmony with themselves, with others, and with the infinite world. On the other hand his choice may be a monorail, deceptive in its speed, single-minded of purpose, and capable of delivering man to his destination: destruction of himself and his world.

Crossroads for teachers no longer present two relatively equally desirable paths to the education of children—one, slow-paced; the other, comfortable and satisfying. In making choices among the variety of directions we choose, it will help to remember the words of Robert E. Lee, who, in other times of crisis, wrote: "The march of Providence is so slow and our desires so impatient, the work of Providence is so immense and our means of aiding it so feeble, the life of humanity is so long and that of the individual so brief, that we often see only the advancing wave and are thus discouraged. It is history that teaches us to hope."

Today, standing at the new crossroads, the directions we take depend upon (1) our ability to recognize our challenges, (2) our ability to meet them, and (3) most of all, our commitment to children.

The challenges facing elementary education are not those alone of the elementary schools.

In a recently completed formal study of schools in changing neighborhoods,[1] schools attained widely varying levels of achievement, as could be expected. In those making the greatest gains, significant clues have been obtained, not only affecting *motivation*, which is the concern of schools for all children, regardless of economic level, but for *teaching processes* which are effective in helping deprived children in their achievement of human relations skills, sensitivities, knowledge and information, and in academic achievement.

The Children Who Get Cheated*

Toni Cade

The education of the nation's young is a crucial subject. And in recent years the public schools have been front-page news. Strikes, riots, disruptions and exposés have revealed deep-rooted problems, have caused seemingly unbridgeable polarizations.

Parents maintain that they are treated as outsiders. Students reject the traditional power relationship of decisions from above and obedience from below. Administrators explain that they are the victims of bad budgets. Books by disenchanted teachers revealing the inadequacies, absurdities and injustices of the system have become popular reading. Many of us, educators and laymen alike, tend to agree that the schools are indeed a mess, that the nation has betrayed its young.

And yet there still are communities across the nation that have kept the faith; that are confident that the professionals know what they are doing, that the morass is merely temporary, that all we need is more money, more time, more patience.

These communities perhaps have good reason to be confident in *their* schools. No matter how trying disruptive students or striking teachers may seem, they still are part of *their* schools. They are white-controlled and white-oriented. They are run by white administrators. They are staffed by white teachers. They are attended by white children learning a white self-concept in the interest of white America. And that should give them some confidence. For isn't the main purpose of an institution the perpetuation of its cultural heritage?

We of the Black community, on the other hand, have no such confidence in your schools. Our memory of being short-changed by these schools is a long one. We have no reason to put our faith in good intentions, experimental solutions, professional know-how. In recent years we have witnessed the muti-

---

* Reprinted by permission from the January 1970 issue of *Redbook*.

lation of too many projects to "upgrade" or "integrate" schools, by bureaucracy or white pressure or sheer incompetence and indifference.

We have been too painfully aware of the damage done to the spirit of our young attending overcrowded classes in dilapidated buildings, trying to learn from obsolete books about the great wars, the great men, the great games, the great lies, taught by a series of middle-class white teachers who come and go in turnstile nonchalance.

The Black community now is moving toward solutions to a problem—the miseducation of our children—that would have provoked bloody warfare in lesser people. In several major cities throughout the country, the Black community has become increasingly adamant in pushing for community control, for we regard the current system of remote control by non-neighborhood whites as a manipulative attempt to keep Black parents invisible, mute and powerless. We have become more and more uncompromising in our demand to participate at the policy-making level in the educational affairs of our children.

More money, more supplies, more experienced staff, an updated curriculum, new buildings, better working conditions for teachers, more adequate counseling services for students—all these promised improvements might result in better schools than now exist. But when you boil it all down, the essential ingredient of education is two-way learning: mutual understanding, mutual respect, dialogue. So most teachers under the present system are, very simply, *incompetent* to teach our children.

They are incompetent because they have too little knowledge of, too little appreciation for and very little professional encouragement to learn about the Black child, his worth, his possibilities. It would be asking too much, perhaps, to expect a white person conditioned by the social mores and myths of this country to have any attitude other than outright racist or paternalistic in dealing with a Black person.

But that is, of course, what we must demand of teachers who come into contact with our children—that they learn to think more clearly and more honestly than they've been trained to, to react more authentically to what they *experience* with the Black student rather than to what they think they *know* of the Black children, to adopt a nonwhite perspective. For what the drive for community control represents, actually, is a long-overdue reaction to the intellectual imperialism of white America, the white control and conditioning of Black minds.

Teachers who wish to teach nonwhite students in locally autonomous districts need to learn about and from the students they teach. They need to realize fully that the "culture of the Negro" is not found in a set of statistics on crime, unemployment, illegitimacy, desertion, welfare payments and unwed mothers; or in the barrage of pseudoscientific material of so-called experts the likes of Nathan Glazer and Daniel Moynihan, authors of *Beyond the Melting Pot,* who, in their ignorance, assert that "the Negro is only an American and nothing else. He has no values and culture to guard and protect."

It is stupid and dangerous and racist to believe that the African-American is the all-American boy next door who grew up with an American Protestant outlook within the traditional Western family, upholding the secular values, the sense of history and the sense of destiny characteristic of European-Americans. It is equally stupid and dangerous to assume that the African-American differs merely because he is not quite up to par; that he is the all-American boy at heart but he's just a little too stupid or a little too poor or a little too uncivilized or a little too ungroomed.

The Black child is none of these. He is simply—different. He acquired the language, religious beliefs, eating habits, notions of common sense, sexual attitudes, concepts of beauty and justice, standards of excellence, responses to pleasure and pain, from the people who raised him—a people with its own mores and traditions.

Well, how, then, does the teacher learn about her Black students? The same way she learns about her nieces, nephews, sons and daughters or other students or people in general—she relates. Unfortunately, the average teacher thinks she already "knows" what "these people" are all about. And what that means in the classroom is—she waters down the material and cannot bring herself to demand excellence from the "poor unfortunates." After all, she imagines, they cannot be expected to tackle complex homework when their IQs are so low and their home conditions are so . . . tsk, tsk . . . dismal.

So the first thing that needs to be understood is—Black people are different. That is a simple fact whose reality the white community and many Negroes still steel themselves against. For the word "different," in this country, carries the connotation "inferior." I recall observing a poor ole geography teacher laboring away to present the Eskimos and Indians as "just like you and me" to her suburban, white, middle-class students. White Americans, bigoted and progressive alike, cannot seem to let go of the presumptuous notion that they are the model everyone wants to emulate.

Back in the days of the integrated-school dream, however, many white Americans were convinced of the difference between European-Americans and Afro-Americans. They were the first to say, Yes, "they" are different, their history is different, even the language they speak and act out is different; "they" ought to stay with their own kind. But suddenly today, as Black people push for their own schools, these same people holler, What's all this "Black" and "different" about? Kids are just kids, after all. Funny business.

The distinguishing features of the Black community are obvious in our literature and music and speech and have for many years attracted the attention of linguists, anthropologists and sociologists. And a few enlightened school boards, with the help of research and study grants, have begun teacher retraining sessions for the purpose of informing teachers of the fact that Mexican-Americans, Filipinos, Puerto Ricans, Afro-Americans, Navahos, et cetera, have a very distinct and rich culture and history of their own: that an understanding of these groups is necessary if the teacher intends to make the educational situation at all real.

An article that appeared in the May 9, 1969, issue of *Time* magazine, titled "Culture: Exploring the Racial Gap," is likely to become part of the seminar material in such teachers' retraining workshops, for it attempts to point out some very crucial differences between the life style of European-Americans and that of African-Americans. It quotes heavily from the work of the late Melville Herskovits, the anthropologist who 28 years ago debunked the theory that "the Negro is a man without a past." Herskovits discussed, for example, the habit among Blacks of dip-eating from the pots and dishes on the stove rather than eating around a table, as is the white ritual. He argued that this habit, like so many others, persists from the communal kitchen custom still prevalent in African villages.

This issue of life-style differences is crucial in education. Consider the traditional lesson of "A Good Diet Consists of the Daily Basic Seven." The white teacher, in speaking of leafy green vegetables, never seems to have heard of collard greens or turnip greens. When she lists the other basic foods, she overlooks beans and rice and other dishes characteristic of the children's homes. The children begin to suspect that something is wrong with their mother's notions of diet. There is nothing wrong at home, necessarily. But something is wrong at school: the white teacher is talking about a white diet only.

This one-sided perspective is what is most criminal and most destructive and what we most object to in the schools. And it is very difficult to awaken white teachers to this fact—as I have learned as a lecturer and consultant. For the experience of most first- and second-generation Europeans in the system—hell-bent on becoming as American and as "mainstream" as possible—assures them that all people are eager to be "mainstream." Not so.

There is, of course, a portion of the Black population that has become trapped by the American Dream and is deluded from time to time into believing that it has "arrived." The Negro who has a middle-class mentality presents no particular problem or challenge to the white teacher. But the so-called Black masses do, for we do not subscribe to white styles. This means teachers of non-mainstream students have got to be sensitive to and knowledgeable about other cultures. But they aren't, and many of our youngsters (as pointed out in recent books on Black children in the schools—*Death at an Early Age*, by Jonathan Kozol, *Our Children Are Dying*, by Nat Hentoff, *36 Children*, by Herbert Kohl) are constantly being chided for being different, for not being like "the nice little children who used to live here before you came."

We are different. Our church services—the dancing, tambourine playing, scream-shout sermons, trances—are alien to the white conception of Protestantism. Our notion of freedom—the liberation of group from the deadly stranglehold of assassins and well-intentioned but ineffective white misfits—is a far cry from your narcissistic impulse to "free" yourself by ripping off your clothes or talking brazenly about sex at cocktail parties. The list is infinite.

The Black child can "put on" if need be. He can trot out the clichés of America the Beautiful if pressed. But he also knows that they are lies. And as he grows up he begins to hate the double life he leads, and hates too those who make it necessary for him to live this double life, this lie. There was a time when Black parents found it necessary to beat their children into submitting to playing the game. But we are no longer willing to squander precious time and energy masquerading as second-rate white folks or good niggers. And we will no longer allow the philosophy of The White Way Is the Right Way to dominate our schools.

There is a particular breed of White Way–Right Way professional who is becoming more and more sought after in the school system. She is the language expert who maintains that she can "correct the ghetto accents" of Black children. She begins with the premise that the language habits of Black children need correcting. Not mastering, but correcting. That the school should *first* learn the language of the children and the community seems never to have been considered. That Negro dialect is a viable language system is not understood. What arrogance! And what destruction this ignorance and arrogance can lead to!

In the *Time* article previously mentioned, an incident worth noting is related. A young Black girl regarded as a chronic nonreader, an illiterate, happened to come across the poem "The Night Before Christmas" written in Negro dialect or some facsimile: "It's the night before Christmas and here in our house, It ain't nothing moving, not even no mouse. . . ." She read it with no difficulty. When handed the original version, she demonstrated all her old reading problems. The linguist who witnessed this began to experiment further along these lines, for it seemed obvious that a great many "problem readers" were problems because they were expected to be able to read a foreign language with facility.

Standard English—the habitual language of the white educated class in this country—is a second language for many groups, and certainly for Black people. White teachers are confronted with the evidence of this every day in the classroom and in Black literature (if they read it), but still can't come to grips with the fact of it. So they persist in telling the Black child he is speaking incorrectly. Negro dialect may not be appropriate in some instances, but it certainly is not incorrect. Standard English is inappropriate in my grandmother's kitchen, but is not incorrect.

"I seen these two dogs in the lot chasing after they own self," relates the student.

" 'I seen these two dogs' is wrong, Johnnie," the teacher begins. " 'I saw these two dogs' is right," she explains impatiently.

As if language had a "right" and "wrong"; as if the presence or absence of standard speech patterns were an ethical issue. Actually it is a political issue; if you want to get ahead in this country, you must master the language of the ruling class. But that does not mean that there is an inherent virtue in the language of that class except the "virtue" of "making it." Standard English communicates with no more drama, color or precision than Negro dialect—considerably less so, as a matter of fact.

Why the obsession with standard English? Why did critics, editors, teachers, go berserk when Merriam-Webster's *Third International Dictionary* was published in 1961? Why is there so little respect for the works of Langston Hughes and others who write in dialect? Because the White Way–Right Way creed is gospel. Because the ruling classes must control and define for all.

The *Third International* does what a dictionary ought to do —it records the language as it is spoken and used and understood by people. Not the "experts," but people. And what is more important—people or form? Actual experience or rigid regulations?

Any teacher who cannot confront my child with some knowledge of who he is and what he is, with some appreciation for his experience and the language he uses to shape and present that experience, is denying my child's humanity and should not be in the classroom.

The Black child should master standard English—not simply to understand Shakespeare and the classics, but also to be able to understand how he is being and has been manipulated by language. The Louisiana State Voter Application is a better argument for his learning standard English than *Macbeth*. But he should also know his own language first.

The fact that dialect persists among college and professional Blacks indicates that there must be some social and psychological satisfaction derived from using it. That the Negro idiom has helped enliven American language indicates its durability and attractiveness. That it is a reflection of the attitudes and experiences of a people means that teachers teaching those people will be severely handicapped without it.

There is nothing wrong with Johnnie or his home or his people or his perceptions when he says, "I seen these two dogs." But there is something wrong with his teacher if she cannot get over the idea that of the two language systems used in the classroom—hers and his—hers is the more appropriate in the classroom setting *at this moment in history.*

What sort of English teacher is it who isn't familiar with the various idioms spoken, written and sung in this country, who isn't aware of the various attitudes among ethnic groups toward the language? An incompetent one. The white community reveres the written word. Ours is a singing strength; we spring from and have maintained an oral tradition. Our manner of communication is largely auditory, kinetic and visual. The "mainstream" manner is primarily literate. I consider Nigeria a Black Republic not only because of its constitution but also because it has revitalized its oral tradition. I will recognize Jamaica as independent and Black not when Jamaicans wave their flag but when they begin to award literary prizes to the dialect authors, when they begin to make use of their dialect dictionary in the class-room.

So to teach Black children in Black-controlled schools, it shall be necessary for white teachers to abandon the White Way–Right Way notion and adopt a new perspective. This requires sensitivity and intelligence, qualities the average teacher sorely lacks, judging from studies maed of public-school personnel.

It takes a fairly conscious person to hear the arrogance in the simple first-grade lesson: Christopher Columbus discovered America. It takes an alert teacher to catch the insidiousness of the Weekly Reader lesson on "The Dark Continent" (like the Dark ages, notice) which contains the statement "South Africa is a developed nation."

Of course, Indians did not write our history books; Africans didn't either. So they are in no position to define. So "history" begins when the white man sets his bloody boot on the land; he "discovers" a continent, a people. And humanists are not in a position to define what is a developed nation or a developed people. The capitalist is in a position to define, and he defines in technological, not humanist, terms. So South Africa is, for all its madness and corruption and criminality, a developed nation.

In *our* schools we shall define the norms, the standards; we shall determine the criteria. For your way won't do.

While white teachers conduct the daily droning of Dick and Jane, little Thelma Watson is thinking about the white families that fled when she and other Black people moved into the neighborhood; she is thinking about her cousins in the South who were spit on and jostled viciously when they tried to go to school after the Supreme Court desegregation decision. She looks at the children in her reader and concludes that they would not even play with her, so why should she read about them?

While the white teachers give lessons on the American Revo-lution and other bloody events in which violence was used to bring about liberation, Joe and Eugene are wondering how come all the warriors they hear about at home, from the Zulu chief Chaka to Malcolm X, are not applauded in class? They too were trying to bring about liberation. And how come white people are forever screaming about violence when Black people demand their rights? And, last: "Well, hell, why don't we Black people declare war?"

Several schools in the Black districts of New York were threatened with closure by the Board of Education for having the nerve to commemorate Malcolm X Memorial Day, February 21st. And yet in many parts of the country our students are expected to join in the celebration of Robert E. Lee's birthday and Confederate Memorial Day.

In *our* schools we shall follow our own calendar, commemorate our own holidays. And if legislators want to debate for the next ten years on the question of whether or not Martin Luther King deserves to be commemorated, that's your business. Of course April 4th is a memorial day for us.

And when the significance of the Fourth of July is discussed, it will not be the grand-opera rhetoric of the Declaration of Independence that will greet our children's ears, but the righteous poetry of Frederick Douglass' "July Fourth and the Negro" oration. For not only is it a better piece of prose, not only is it a more honest document, but also it is a far more pertinent piece for us and for these times, for it raised a question in the 1850s that has yet to be answered: What have I (the Black man, the nonfree) to do with your national independence? By assuming that I should join in the jubilee, is not America false to its past and present?

The kinds of changes—redefinitions, re-evaluations—that we must bring about in our children's schools are voluminous. But a few simple illustrations are worth presenting here to clarify what is meant by non-White Way–Right Way outlook.

Clearly the "glorious days of the Empire" would be defined from a Black perspective as an adventure in rape, plunder, pillage, enslavement and slander of non-white peoples. The "tragedy of Little Big Horn" was simply the justifiable execution of a handful of scruffy little empire builders and greedy adventurers who hustled the legal inhabitants, the Indians, once too often. The pastoral Dixie plantation days, depicted in a great many American history texts as idyllic, would have to be supplemented by studies of slave treatment and slave revolts.

The Reconstruction period will certainly not be overlooked, as it is in most textbooks, but taught as a Black period—a period in which free Black men passed very useful legislation (such as free public-school education for all). The grand slogans of the "Great Wars," such as "A War to Make the World Safe for Democracy," will be investigated and the real causes will be examined: partition of Africa, imperialism, competition between the "Great Powers" for the loot.

And a great many Black Americans will be exhumed to get a composite, rather than piecemeal, picture of America—inventors, artists, statesmen, writers, orators, warriors. We have been Marion Anderson-ed and George Washington Carver-ed to death. Those two do not disturb the "order" of the white mentality (unless we look closely at how Carver was swindled out of his money) ; they do not upset the traditional lie. Resurrecting the Black men and women who have shaped the reality of this country, who have been murdered by white historians, novelists and other taxidermists, is going to upset people's minds. It's inevitable. Perhaps very necessary. Certainly long overdue.

The task that faces us, the Black community, is not to destroy the myths for the sake of iconoclasm but for the purpose of telling the truth, for too little truth is told in this country. And information and truth are the most valuable tools for our survival. Our task is not to blow up the schools or demolish the system or dismiss the material already in existence—but, rather, to re-interpret, redefine, redesign; to question the assumptions that have too long been palmed off as "history," to investigate the illusions too long palmed off as "reality." Isn't that what education is: investigation, inquiry?

We do not accomplish all this by going to school, by merely occupying chairs. We occupy Harlem, Watts, Oakland—but we do not define phenomena there; we do not control them. And that is what we must do. For in many ways control of the schools is control of the self, control of one's destiny.

Whenever the subject of community control is discussed at public meetings, white participants predictably raise several issues: Isn't integration a better solution to the problem? Community control sounds like "separatism"—isn't that reverse racism? How are you going to get control of your schools when the teachers' union is not behind you? And there's always some-one bound to scream: If you're so dissatisfied with this country, why don't you leave?

What is the point of leaving the country; where is there to go? White power, through the Yankee dollar, propaganda, corpo-ration and government agents and the Peace Corps, has annexed the earth. At least here the manipulative strings are visible. I, for one, prefer visible control to remote control. Besides, this is my home. My people built it and paid for it in blood and breath. And I am sure that my children will inherit this earth, in spite of their lack of humility.

Integration — what does it mean? If we mean an open soci-ety, an equal sharing of social and material advantages, a plu-ralistic society whose groups are volutarily and enthusiastically bound to a corporate future — it's never happened. Why expect it of the schools?

"Integrated," for you, means you tolerate my presence under your control. Real integration means co-operation and sharing, including sharing of power. In our schools integration would mean intermingling of various idioms (African, Asian, Indian, European, Hispanic) that make up this country. Your "integra-tion" as a social or educational goal simply wields no power and yields no truth.

It is inevitable that the Black community fighting for the very same powers of districting and control that rural townships across the country take for granted will be charged with "re-verse racism" (as opposed to the forward-thrust, third-gear, white brand of racism). We would do well to remember that racism is not merely an attitude but a behavior in operation. And it should then seem absurd even to use the phrase "Black racism," for the simple reason that no matter how we may mistrust you or even hate you, we can't keep you out of apartments, out of jobs, out of churches, out of hospitals, out of history books, out of touch with your past or yourselves or away from the levers of power. And nowhere have I seen or heard the statement that the Black community intends to cut itself off from any resources, skills, experiences, ideas or people that would help create good schools. Whites evidently hear something else; if they aren't asked to be the drivers, they assume they can't be riders either.

Of course it is very clear that Black control of any kind is a great threat to the white man's sense of order. In New York City, for example, the so-called Decentralization Bill, which became law in April, 1969, "recentralizes" rather than "decentralizes"; the power to propose texts and teaching materials, the power to overrule, suspend and oust local school governing boards, still remains in the hands of those outside the community. Hierarchical domination is retained.

Yet there were — and still are — many excellent blueprints for community control. The New York state legislature chose to ignore one of these in favor of the law mentioned above. Roy Innis and Victor Solomon, of National CORE, drafted a plan for an independent Harlem school system. It would be chartered by the New York state legislature and would be directly responsible to the state, just as other systems throughout the state are. Harlem would negotiate its own contracts for staff, maintenance and suppliers, just as other districts do. The Harlem school district could decentralize into subdistricts for greater community involvement and efficiency, just as the law allows other districts to do. The system would be funded by city, state and Federal governments in much the same way as the current central system is funded, except that the money would go directly to the Harlem district.

In short, the board of the independent Harlem school system would in no way differ from the hundreds of school boards in the state, except perhaps that it might not have the power to impose taxes and so would probably invite foundations and private industry to supplement the support. The CORE blueprint, like other decentralization blueprints, simply seeks the same power as that possessed by every suburban or rural township in the state if not in the country.

A Black board contracting for the maintenance and construction of Black schools? Well, we all know the ethnic make-up of the construction unions throughout the country. We all know how many picket lines, how many threats, are needed to get one or two token minority members into the construction unions. As for maintenance — out of 945 custodians in the New York City schools, only 35 are Black. So this aspect alone is too radical for white America.

The idea of a Black board's purchasing its own texts and school supplies will cause publishing houses to tremble. They'll have to stop pussyfooting about and hire Black editors by the truckload. To give the power of hiring and firing teachers to a Black board has already caused a seemingly unbridgeable split between teachers and community. And that is a pity. For there are few alternatives to community control of public schools.

There are, of course, many Black neighborhood storefront schools throughout the country that were established as a result of the Freedom School campaign launched in the early '60s in the South by SNCC, CORE and other organizations.

In New York there are the storefront Street Academies, which the New York Urban League established with funds from the Ford Foundation and private corporations to attract our dropouts. But the academies cannot at the moment service all of our children.

There are private schools and boarding schools, but not every Black family wants or can afford to send its children to them. The so-called Black Muslims' University of Islam (elementary and secondary schools) is still functioning and accepting applications in Chicago, Detroit, New York, Washington, D.C., Atlanta, Miami, Los Angeles and 80 other cities. But not all Afro-Americans are sympathetic to its teachings. So we are also pushing for neighborhood schools. There are many alternatives to Head Start but there are few alternatives to community-run public schools.

In 1968 the CBS telecast of the series "Of Black America" brought to light a particular kind of preschool currently being set up in the Black community by Black parents. The Freedom Library Day School in Philadelphia, founded in 1967 by John Churchville, was one of the subjects of the first program of the series. The segment of the TV program on the school opened on a well-lighted classroom furnished with movable chairs, tables and blackboard. The children were receiving a lesson in selfhood and self-defense. This is approximately how it proceeded:

"What do you want?" the teacher asked.

"Freedom," the children answered.

"Okay, okay, you can have it next year."

"No, now," they demanded. "We want it now."

"What are you?" the teacher asked.

"Afro-Americans," came the vigorous reply.

The teacher then singled out one of the boys and in utter seriousness and with absolute authority told him, "You are a Negro and you are three years old."

"No," the child insisted, a little uncomfortable about contradicting an elder but confident he was right. "I'm an Afro-American and I'm four."

The teacher demanded that he step forward. The little boy did, somewhat hesitantly. The teacher pulled out a dollar bill and offered it to the boy if he would say he was three and a Negro and if he would agree to wait for his freedom. The child paused, gritted his teeth, shook his head.

"No!" he shouted. "I'm four years old and I'm Afro-American. And I want my freedom now," he insisted.

The directors of these pregrade schools are perfectly aware that pride in the self and confidence come not solely through Swahili courses or through race glorification but also through accomplishment, mastery of material, the acquisition of skills. After the selfhood lesson the teacher at the Freedom Library Day School began conducting a course in new math, and the three- and four-year-olds were having no difficulty whatever.

The directors of these neighborhood schools throughout the country are aware, too, that the Black child needs certain armor, a sure grasp of his self, before he is ready to move into the merciless arena of the public schools. Head Start programs do not, for my money, toughen the child. They simply expose him sooner to the process of conditioning him to meet the social expectations of White America.

Schools like Churchville's are more vital than can be expressed. Not only is the child taught a sense of his self, not only does he learn to protect himself against arbitrary white authority, but also he is taught to produce, how to acquire skills, to master subject matter. If there is anything that characterizes the white teachers I know in nurseries, in grade schools, in college-prep programs like Discovery and SEEK, it is their inability even to expect the Black student to do well. And so the white teacher, under the present system, is inadequate and incompetent, and will remain so until Black parents are in a position to impress upon her the need to do her homework.

And it is clear that the split between the teachers and the community — both unaware that all along they have been agitating for the same thing, quality education — did prevent, and in days to come will prevent, the passage of any sound community-control bill. So it is clear that bloody days are ahead. For Black parents are determined that no incompetent teacher has the right to play with the hearts and minds of our young, no matter what "due process" protection is guaranteed by traditional trade-union politics. And white Americans have difficulty understanding that they will have to let go of their tyrannical notion that only whites can and should have any power.

In the late 1950s, when the streets of London ran red with the blood of West Indians and Africans whose very presence in the country, whose simple wish to live as human beings, began to disturb the sleep of the white man, my Pakistani landlady, who knows the British all too well, calmly poured my cup of tea and said: "They are losing their empire, so they are losing their minds."

Target for the 70's*
The Right to Read

The former U.S. Commissioner of Education James E. Allen, Jr. appearing before the General Subcommittee on Education of the U.S. House of Representatives Committee on Education and Labor

Chairman Pucinski,   Commissioner Allen, we are very pleased to have you here this morning. As you know, our subcommittee has

---

* *American Education* (December, 1969), 11-14.

started a series of hearings on the educational needs of elementary and secondary schools for the 70's. . . . We are hopeful that from these hearings can come information and opinions that will give all of us the chance to look down-range the next 10 years to anticipate the problems and the needs of our schools and to do something meaningful about them. It seems to me one of the great problems we have had in education is that we are always chasing the problem instead of anticipating it.

Dr. Allen, Thank you very much. Mr. Chairman and members of the committee. I am delighted for this opportunity to appear before you to discuss matters of very deep concern to our Nation and to all of us in the field of education. . . . We in the Office of Education, Department of Health, Education, and Welfare, are presently working on a statement of goals for the 70's. We would welcome the opportunity to discuss the statement with you when we have completed it.

This morning I would like to bring to your attention one of these problems, so grave in its import for our Nation that it must, in my judgment, receive immediate attention. I refer to our failure in the teaching of reading, a failure that can no longer be tolerated.

In an address two weeks ago before the annual meeting of the National Association of State Boards of Education, I called upon the educational and lay leaders of America to join me in a nationwide effort to see to it that by the end of the 1970's no boy or girl shall be leaving our schools without the skill and the desire to read to the full limits of his capability.

Imagine, if you can, what life would be like if you could not read, or if your reading skills were so meager as to limit you to the simplest of writings, and if for you the door to the whole world of knowledge and the inspiration available through the printed word had never opened.

For more than a quarter of our population this is true. For them education, in a very important way, has been a failure, and they stand as a reproach to all of us who hold in our hands the shaping of the opportunity for education. These individuals have been denied a right — a right as fundamental as the right to life, liberty, and the pursuit of happiness — the right to read.

Education has come to mean many things and to encompass a wide range of information and experience, but certainly it must still include, as it did in the beginning, the ability to read. Those who do not gain this ability in the course of their early education lack a skill necessary to all other areas of learning and are being denied a fundamental educational right.

From a variety of statistical information accumulated by the Office of Education regarding reading deficiencies throughout the country, these shocking facts stand out:

One out of every four students nationwide has significant reading deficiencies.

In large city school systems up to half of the students read below expectation. For example, toward the end of the period during which I was Commissioner of Education in New York, we measured reading in the State and found that 46 percent of the sixth-graders in the City of New York were reading well below the minimum State competency level.

There are more than 3 million illiterates in our adult population.

About half of the unemployed youth, ages 16-21, are functionally illiterate.

Three quarters of the juvenile offenders in New York City are two or more years retarded in reading. I am sure similar statistics would apply to other cities.

In a recent U.S. Armed Forces program called Project 100,-000, 68.2 percent of the young men fell below grade seven in reading and academic ability.

The tragedy of these statistics is that they represent a barrier to success that for many young adults produces the misery of a life marked by poverty, unemployment, alienation, and, in many cases, crime.

It must be recognized also, however, that for the majority who do not acquire the basic reading skills, there can be another barrier which limits the fulfillment of their right to read. This barrier exists when the skill of reading is not accompanied by the desire to read. We fail, therefore, just as much in assuring the right to read when a student's desire is absent as when his skills are missing.

It is inexcusable that in this day when man has achieved such giant steps in the development of his potential, when many of his accomplishments approach the miraculous, there still should be those who cannot read.

It is my view, therefore, that there is no higher nationwide priority in the field of education than the provision of the right to read for all, and that the Office of Education and the Department of Health, Education, and Welfare can do no greater service for the cause of education than to spearhead a nationwide attack to eliminate this failure of our education effort. It is my belief that we should immediately set for ourseves the goal of assuring that by the end of the 1970's the right to read shall be a reality for all — that no one shall be leaving our schools without the skill and the desire necessary to read to the full limits of his capability.

Chapter Five

Housing

Everyone wants a decent place to live. The place we live in and the general neighborhood in which we dwell says much about our total life style. Not all Americans have what we would consider to be the basic necessities for a decent home. Not everyone has hot and cold running water and indoor plumbing. Census figures clearly bear this out.

However, you need not travel to a remote rural community to find these conditions. Many of our worse slums, characterized by conditions that simply do not allow for basic human needs, are urban. Rat bites are common in slum housing. Lack of necessary heat in winter and hot water for bathing are frequently reported. Even our newer urban renewal projects suffer from deficiencies.

The problem of adequate housing is serious. Urban renewal projects destroy poor housing, but rarely are sufficient new units built to accommodate the displaced. Put out of their homes, the displaced residents go farther into the slums to seek housing.

The Department of Housing and Urban Development has made a beginning, but only a beginning. A national commitment to decent housing for every family is essential for our country.

The Dimension of Need*

How numerous are the ill-housed in America? How many dwellings are below an acceptable standard of decency? These fundamental questions, of course, must be answered before present national housing efforts can be evaluated and new ones planned. They were the first order of inquiry for both Presidential study groups.

The Douglas Commission came away from its attempt to find answers, clearly annoyed with the lack of data about the rate of housing deterioration and facts on which policy recommendations could be based.

There has been no satisfactory analysis of present housing needs and a similar estimate of probable future needs as guides for housing policy and programs. Aside from the hazards in predicting birth and fertility rates, the basic facts for such studies, in reasonable detail and refinement, are not available. In some respects this is the most damning indictment against the public concern, including but by no means limited to governmental concern, with housing in this country.

There are not even good working definitions of a decent home and suitable living environment, the supposed anchor points of our national housing goal, used in what statistics are being gathered. Still more elusive, therefore, are the complex questions such as the following:

· How many presently acceptable houses will slide into the substandard category through the ravages of age, neglect, and shifting land uses?

· How many presently substandard houses could be made acceptable through rehabilitation?

· What is the best balance between public and private investment in housing?

The only reasonably comprehensive data on housing conditions or quality are those of the Bureau of the Census. To say

---

* Prepared by Urban America, Inc. for the League of Women Voters of the United States. Reprinted with permission.

that the available data are inadequate is no adverse criticism of the bureau, which has worked hard and intelligently on housing. A nationwide, decennial census, however, cannot supply the complete range of facts needed to judge housing quality. The bureau knows this perfectly well. Its 1960 Census of Housing says:

"The combination of data on condition and plumbing facilities is considered one measure of housing quality. It takes account of the physical characteristics of the unit — the structural condition and the presence of basic plumbing facilities (water supply, toilet facilities, and bathing facilities). Although such factors as light, ventilation, and neighborhood also reflect quality, particularly in urban areas, it is not feasible to measure them in a large-scale census enumeration. These elements, however, ties."

often are closely associated with condition and plumbing facili-

The limited role of the large-scale census enumeration stems not only from its general focus that omits specific details. Major difficulties include these:

• The term structural condition is confusing. It does not refer to the basic fabric of the building. Rather it looks to "visible defects ... associated with weather tightness, extent of disrepair, hazards to physical safety of the occupants, and inadeuate or makeshift constructions."

• The census item of piped hot water is misleading because the plumbing facilities are not necessarily in the dwelling unit. The proper item is piped hot water inside the structure. It may not be in the dwelling unit. And even there, the hot water may be supplied "only at certain times of the day, week, or year."

• Omitted items of light, ventilation, and neighborhood are crucial to housing quality. Dual egress, in some parts of the country installed heating facilities, size of rooms and dwelling units, also crucial, are left out.

• And the census belief in a correlation between those quality items enumerated and those not enumerated is questionable.

The [Douglas] Commission warns against the common tendency to read into the census housing data more than is there. Visible condition of building (which the census classifies as sound, deteriorating, and dilapidated) and plumbing facilities are indeed, as the census puts it, in combination "one measure of housing quality," but only one — and a crude one at that. Quite surely it is on the conservative side — i.e., it results in a lower estimate of the volume of substandard housing than most reasonable persons would arrive at on the basis of careful local studies. This seems doubly likely for the housing in older, large, central cities and industrial suburbs of metropolitan areas. The census definition amounts to "a nearly weathertight box with pipes in it," and this notion of quality, unfortunately, is hopelessly inadequate.

In short, the hard job of estimating and projecting housing needs is made all but impossible by the ridiculously inadequate data now at hand. Nearly everyone concerned with the subject has known and said this since the first Census of Housing was published in 1940, more than a quarter of a century ago. Yet these same critics of the data have gone ahead to use, revise, and manipulate these statistics (and often others, that are worse) to produce elaborate and rickety structures of partial or misleading facts. Personal guesses and far-fetched assumptions with little relation to the actual world around us clutter the housing and urban problems field.

The Commission had to content itself with the available data. But in a series of hearings around the country, from testimony and direct investigation, the Commission reached the conclusion that the data had to be regarded as conservative in portraying housing inadequacy.

There are today at the very least 11 million substandard and overcrowded dwelling units in the United States. This is 16 percent of the total housing inventory. According to the census, three-fifths of all that substandard housing is said to be in rural areas — generally on farms and in towns of less than 2,500 persons. Thirty-six per cent of all rural housing is substandard, compared with estimates of 10 per cent of all urban housing. These are highly conservative figures. And they not only greatly understate the problem but tend to mask the critical aspect of the urban housing problem — the concentration of substandard housing and of poor people.

In metropolitan areas, there are about four million substandard and overcrowded units. Almost that many more are so deteriorated they need constant repair. Another several million have serious code violations. Recent surveys in some inner-city slums indicate, instead of improvement, a deterioration in this inventory. Not all of the people in these houses are poor. Many have moderate incomes — between $3,500 and $6,000 — and are trapped in inadequate housing because there was no decent housing within their ability to pay. It should also be noted that just as all who live in bad housing are not poor, neither do all poor people live in bad housing.

In some places, there is a steady increase in substandard housing. In New York City, for example the number of substandard units has risen since 1960. However, it is not only the size but the concentration of substandard urban housing which is the problem in city areas. In cities where the general average for substandard over-crowded units in only 10 percent, 40 per cent of the housing in slum areas may be deficient.

Housing inadequacy is concentrated not just by area, but in its impact on specific categories of people. The point is worth dwelling on, because a persistent source of confusion in housing analyses is the contrast between the visible problems and what statistics portray as aggregate national progress. The Douglas Commission itself sponsored a study by Dr. Frank S. Kristol of New York City's Housing and Development Administration, which spoke of "unprecedented achievements" in improving housing quality since 1950. The extent of these "achievements," as the Commission has noted, depends on how one reads the available figures and the standards on which they are based. The achievements have also been highly selective, largely bypassing two particular groups. The first, as the Douglas Commission points out, is the poor.

Perhaps the most pertinent facts about poverty and housing are the following:

1. For the whole United States, 19 per cent of all housing units were substandard in 1960. Of the units occupied by poor households, 36 per cent were substandard.

2. Of all owner-occupied units in the United States, 11 per cent were substandard. Of those whose owners were poor, 30 per cent were substandard.
3. Of all renter-occupied units in the United States, 23 per cent were substandard. Of those whose renters were poor, 42 per cent were substandard.
4. For all SMSAs [Standard Metropolitan Statistical Areas], 11 per cent of all housing units were substandard in 1960. Of those units occupied by poor families, 23 per cent were substandard.
5. Of all owner-occupied units in SMSAs, 5 per cent were substandard; of those whose owners were poor, 14 per cent were substandard.
6. Of all renter-occupied units in SMSAs, 16 per cent were substandard; of those whose renters were poor, 30 per cent were substandard.

Thus in these six key comparisons, the proportions of poor households in substandard housing is about twice the proportion for all households — poor and not poor — in four cases, and almost three times in two of the comparisons.

Others may be puzzled at first, as was the Commission, that the percentage of the poor in substandard housing does not seem especially high. Only in item number three — all poor renters in the United States — did the proportion approach one-half. But, as stressed earlier, the figures are based on a primitive definition of substandard housing; they do not refer to merely poor housing, but only to the rock-bottom stratum of utterly unfit housing.

Further, the proportions seem impossible to those who hold the common belief that families usually pay 20 to 25 per cent of their income for housing. Many estimates of housing needs are based on this rule of thumb, but it does not hold true. The widespread gap in rent-income ratios by income class is dramatized by the following exceptionally useful information from Mr. Kristof's housing-needs study for the Commission:

• Of renters with incomes under $2,000 in 1960 . . . 90 per cent pay 25 per cent or more of income for rent, and of these . . . 13 per cent pay 25 to 35 per cent of income for rent; 77 per cent pay 35 per cent or more of income for rent.

• Of renters with incomes between $2,000 and $3,000 in 1960 . . . 63 per cent pay 25 per cent or more of income for rent, and of these . . . 31 per cent pay 25 to 35 per cent of income for rent; 32 per cent pay 35 per cent or more of income for rent.

• Of renters with incomes between $6,000 and $7,000 in 1960 . . . 6 per cent pay 25 per cent or more for rent; 1 per cent pay 35 per cent or more for rent.

• Of renters with incomes over $8,000 in 1960 . . . 1 per cent pay 25 to 35 per cent of income for rent; 0.5 per cent pay 35 per cent or more of income for rent.

Clearly, if many poor households escape rock-bottom bad housing, there is little comfort to be drawn from these facts, indicating as they do that such escape can only mean cruelly curtailed expenditures for other basic necessities such as food, clothing, or medical care. While no comparable figures are available for poor owner-occupiers, presumably those who keep out of substandard quarters also do so at the expense of other necessities.

There are thus families of marginal income who, as Anthony Downs has said, are more "housing poor" than "money poor." The lower the income, the higher the "housing tax" they pay in terms of a disproportionate outlay for shelter.

An additional "tax" is paid by minority groups, the second population segment bypassed by housing progress. The financial burden of being black was documented by the National Advisory Commission on Civil Disorders.

Negroes in large cities are often forced to pay the same rents as whites and receive less for their money, or pay higher rents for the same accommodations.

The first type of discriminatory effect — paying the same amount but receiving less — is illustrated by data from the 1960 Census for Chicago and Detroit.

In certain Chicago census tracts, both whites and nonwhites paid median rents of $88, and the proportions paying various specific rents below that median were almost identical. But the units rented by nonwhites were typically:

• Smaller (the median number of rooms was 3.35 for nonwhites versus 3.95 for whites).

· In worse condition (30.7 per cent of all nonwhite units were deteriorating or dilapidated units versus 11.6 per cent for whites).

· Occupied by more people (the median household side was 3.53 for nonwhites versus 2.88 for whites).

· More likely to be overcrowded (27.4 per cent of nonwhite units had 1.01 or more persons per room versus 7.9 per cent for whites).

In Detroit, whites paid a median rental of $77 as compared to $76 among nonwhites. Yet 27 per cent of nonwhite units were deteriorating or dilapidated, as compared to only 10.3 per cent of all white units.

The second type of discriminatory effect — paying more for similar housing — is illustrated by data from a study of housing conditions in disadvantaged neighborhoods in Newark, N.J. In four areas of that city... nonwhites with housing essentially similar to that of whites paid rents that were from 8.1 per cent to 16.8 per cent higher. Though the typically larger size of nonwhite households, with consequent harder wear and tear, may partially justify the differences in rental, the study found that nonwhites were paying a definite "color tax" of apparently well over 10 per cent on housing. This condition prevails in most racial ghettos.

The combination of high rents and low incomes forces many Negroes to pay an excessively high proportion of their income for housing.

The high proportion of income that must go for rent leaves less money in such households for other expenses. Undoubtedly, this is a major reason many Negro households regard housing as one of their worst problems.

The Douglas Commission offered further evidence of the impact of race on housing quality.

1. In metropolitan areas in 1960, 23.5 per cent of all poverty households, white and nonwhite, lived in substandard housing (by the definition of substandard we are forced to use).

2. In the same areas in the same year, 18.9 per cent of white households below the poverty line lived in substandard housing.

3. In the same areas in the same year, 41.6 per cent of non-white

households below the poverty line lived in substandard housing.
4. In other words, within the poverty category, the proportion
of Negroes and other nonwhites in substandard housing was
more than twice the proportion among whites. Race, therefore,
seems to be a significant factor in bad housing.

The analyses above deal with the past and present. What of
the future of housing in America? What must the nation do to
meet the needs of the ill-housed?

The officially adopted goals of the Housing Act of 1968 were
drawn from the work of the Kaiser Committee. In its final report, the Committee summarizes the present situation, looks to
future growth, and arrives at some large and challenging figures.

A study for this Committee by TEMPO, General Electric's
Advanced Studies Center, estimated the current number of
"lower-income families" for whom a "decent home" is still un-
affordable (the "noneffective demand" in the U.S. housing market) :

• About 7.8 million American families — one in every eight
— cannot now afford to pay the market price for standard housing that would cost no more than 20 per cent of their total incomes. (The average ratio of housing costs to gross income for
the total population is 15 per cent.)

• About half of these 7.8 million families are surviving on
less than $3,000 a year — the federal poverty level.

The study projected the size of this gap 10 years from now,
assuming no marked changes in current economic trends, national policies, and priorities among federal programs. The pro-
jection showed that the prevalence of poverty can be expected
to decline only slightly:

In 1978, about 7.5 million families — one in every 10 — would
still be unable to afford standard housing. . . .

What happens to the millions of families too poor to afford
decent housing? Part of the answer is apparent in Harlem,
Cleveland's Hough District, Chicago's Lawndale, other central
cities' slums, and the shanties of rural poverty areas.

TEMPO's estimate of the characteristics and conditions of the
nation's total housing inventory suggests a fuller picture. There
are about 66 million housing units and 60 million households.

Although there appear to be more than enough rooftops:

· An estimated 6.7 million occupied units are substandard dwellings — four million lacking indoor plumbing and 2.7 million in dilapidated condition;

· 6.1 million units (both standard and substandard) are overcrowded with more than one person per room;

· Among the six million vacant units, only about two million are in standard condition and available for occupancy — the nation's lowest available vacancy rate since 1958.

These estimates suggest a growing shortage of decent housing, not only for lower-income families but for the entire population.

A World of Trouble:
The Pruitt-Igoe Housing Project*

Lee Rainwater

The Pruitt-Igoe Housing Project is in St. Louis. Built in 1954, the project was the first high-rise public housing in the city. It consists of 33 eleven-story slab-shaped buildings designed to provide housing for about 2800 families. At present, it houses about 10,000 Negroes in 2,000 households. What started out as a precedent-breaking project to improve the lives of the poor in St. Louis, a project hailed not only by the local newspapers but by *Architectural Forum,* has become an embarrassment to all concerned. In the last few years the project has at all times had a vacancy rate of over 20 percent. News of crime and accidents in the project makes a regular appearance in the newspapers, and the words "Pruitt-Igoe" have become a household term — in

* Copyright by National Affairs, Inc. 1967. Reprinted by permission of *The Public Interest* and the author.

lower class Negro homes as well as in the larger community —
for the worst in ghetto living.

The description of Pruitt-Igoe which follows and the implications drawn, are based on a three-year study which I, together
with a dozen colleagues, have been conducting. Pruitt-Igoe is not
offered as typical of slum conditions in the ghetto — no other
public housing project in the country approaches it in terms of
vacancies, tenant concerns and anxieties, physical deterioration.
Rather, Pruitt-Igoe is interesting precisely because it condenses
into one 57-acre tract all of the problems and difficulties that
arise from race and poverty, and all of the impotence, indifference, and hostility with which our society has so far dealt with
these problems. Processes that are sometimes beneath the sur-
face in less virulent slums are readily apparent in Pruitt-Igoe.
And because Pruitt-Igoe exists as one kind of Federal Government response to the problems of poverty, the failure of that
response is worth contemplating.

The Dumping Ground

Pruitt-Igoe houses families for which our society seems to
have no other place. The original tenants were drawn very heavily from several land-clearance areas in the inner city. Although
there were originally some white tenants (Igoe was built for
whites, Pruitt for Negroes, but a Supreme Court decision outlaw-
ing segregated public housing resulted in an "integrated" project in its earlier years), all of the whites have moved out and the
population is now all Negro. Only those Negroes who are des-
perate for housing are willing to live in Pruitt-Igoe — over half
of the households are headed by women and over half derive
their principal income from public assistance of one kind or another. The project has proved particularly unappealing to "average" families, that is, families in which there is both a mother
and father and a small number of children. Thus, while the overall vacancy rate has run between 20 and 25 percent for several
years, the vacancy rate in two-bedroom apartments has been in
the 35–40 percent range.

Life in Pruitt-Igoe, and in the St. Louis ghetto generally, is not quite as flamboyant as in Harlem, but it has the same essential characteristics. As sociologists have discovered each time they have examined a particular lower class community in detail, the lower class lives in "a world of trouble."

In the slum, people are continually confronted with dangers from both human and non-human sources. Public housing removes some of the non-human sources of danger (like rats or faulty electrical wiring), but can replace them by others, as when children fall out of windows or into elevator shafts in Pruitt-Igoe's high-rise buildings, or burn themselves on exposed steam pipes, or cut themselves on the broken glass outside. After about two years of intensive field observation in the Pruitt-Igoe project, our research team administered a questionnaire to a representative sample of tenants to discover how extensive were some of the difficulties we had noticed. Let me list some of the troubles which over half of this representative sample of tenants characterized as "a very big problem" in the project.

A few of these problems had to do with the design and maintenance of the project:

There's too much broken glass and trash around outside.

The elevators are dangerous.

The elevators don't stop on every floor, so many people have to walk up or down to get to their apartments.

There are mice and cockroaches in the buildings.

People use the elevators and halls to go to the bathroom.

However, by far the greatest number of troubles that people complained about had as much to do with the behavior of their follow tenants as it did with design and maintenance problems *per se:*

Bottles and other dangerous things get thrown out of windows and hurt people.

People who don't live in the project come in and make a lot of trouble with fights, stealing, drinking and the like.

People don't keep the area around the incinerator clean.

The laundry rooms aren't safe: clothes get stolen and people get attacked.

The children run wild and cause all kinds of damage.

People use the stairwells and laundry rooms for drinking and things like that.

A woman isn't safe in the halls, stairways or elevators.

Given these kinds of experiences it's hardly surprising that, although the great majority of the tenants feel that their *apartments* are better than their previous dwelling units, only a minority demonstrate any real attachment to the project community, and most would very much like to move out to a neighborhood that would be nicer and safer.

It is understandable that a good many of them develop a rather jaundiced view of the public housing program. Thus, when we asked tenants what the government was trying to accomplish by building public housing and how well this had in fact been accomplished, we got answers like these:

"They were trying to put a whole bunch of people in a little bitty space. They did a pretty good job — there's a lot of people here."

"They were trying to better poor people (but) they tore down one slum and built another; put all kinds of people together; made a filthy place and so on."

"They were trying to get rid of the slum, but they didn't accomplish too much. Inside the apartment they did, but not outside."

Other troubles also make life difficult for the project tenants. For example, we asked our sample to indicate from a list of various kinds of aggressive and deviant behaviors how serious and how frequent they felt such behavior to be. One cluster of items turned out to be judged by the tenants as both highly serious and very frequent (over half of the people characterizing these behaviors as very frequent):

Holding somebody up and robbing them.

Being a wino or alcoholic.

Stealing from somebody.

Teenagers yelling curse words at adults.

Breaking windows.

Drinking a lot and fooling around on the streets.

Teenagers getting in fights.

Boys or girls having sexual relations with a lot of different
boys or girls.

In short, though some social scientists have quarreled with
Kenneth Clark's emphasis on the "tangle of pathology" in the
ghetto, it would seem that at least this sample from one federally-
supported ghetto shares his views.

The Lower Class Adaptation

The observer who examines the lower class community in any
detail perceives an almost bewildering variety of difficulties that
confront its inhabitants. But if one wishes to move from simple
observation to understanding and on to practical action, it is
necessary to bring some order into this chaos of troubles, problems, pains, and failure. That is, one must move from a description of *what* lower class life is like to an understanding of *why*
it is that way.

Let us start with an inventory of behavior in the lower class
community that middle class people think of as hallmarks of the
"tangle of pathology" of slum and ghetto worlds:

High rates of school dropouts.

Poor school accomplishment for those who do stay in.

Difficulties in establishing stable work habits on the part of
those who get jobs.

High rates of dropping out of the labor force.

Apathy and passive resistance in contacts with people who
are "trying to help" (social workers, teachers, etc.)

Hostility and distrust toward neighbors.

Poor consumer skills — carelessness or ignorance in the use
of money.

High rates of mental illness.

Marital disruptions and female-headed homes.

Illegitimacy.

Child abuse or indifference to children's welfare.

Property and personal crimes.

Dope addiction, alcoholism.

Destructiveness and carelessness toward property, one's own
and other people's.

All of this behavior is highly disturbing to middle class people — and most of it is even more disturbing to the lower class people who must live with it. It is not necessary to assume that all lower class families engage in even some of these practices to regard such practices as hallmarks of the pathology of the lower class world. Lower class people are forced to live in an invironment in which the probability of either becoming involved in such behavior, or being the victim of it, is much higher than it is in other kinds of neighborhoods. From the point of view of social epidemiology, then, this is a high-risk population.

Behavior of this kind is very difficult for most middle class observers to understand. If, however, this behavior is seen in the context of the ways of life lower class people develop in order to cope with their punishing and depriving milieu, then it becomes much easier to understand. Much of the social science research dealing with lower class life in general, or with particular forms of deviant behavior such as juvenile delinquency, has sought to place these kinds of behavior in their contexts. As a result of these studies, we now understand that the "unreasonable" behavior which so often perplexes outsiders generally arises as a logical extension of the styles of life that are available to lower class people in their efforts to adapt to their world.

The ways people live represent their efforts to cope with the predicaments and opportunities that they find in the world as they experience it. The immediately experienced world of lower class adults presents them with two kinds of problems:

1. They are not able to find enough money to live in what they, and everyone else, would regard as the average American way. Because of inability to find work or only work at very low pay, they learn that the best they can hope for if they are "sensible" is despised housing, an inferior diet, a very few pleasures.

2. Because of their poverty, they are constrained to live among other individuals similarly situated — individuals who, the experience of their daily lives teaches them, are dangerous, difficult, out to exploit or hurt them in petty or significant ways. And they learn that in their communities they can expect only poor and inferior service and protection from such

institutions as the police, the courts, the schools, the sanitation department, the landlords, and the merchants.

It is to this world that they must adapt. Further, as they grow up, they learn from their experience with those around them that persons such as they can expect nothing better. From infancy on, they begin to adapt to that world in ways that allow them to sustain themselves — but at the same time often interfere with the possibility of adapting to a different world, should such a different world become available to them. Thus, in Pruitt-Igoe, eight-year-old girls are quite competent to inform the field worker that boys and men are no damn good, are not to be trusted, and that it isn't necessary to listen to or obey your mother because she's made such a mess of her life.

We know form sociological studies of unemployment that even stable middle or working class persons are likely to begin to show some of these lower class adaptive techniques under the stress of long-term unemployment. In the lower class itself, there is never a question of responding to the stress of sudden deprivation, since a depriving world is often all that the individual ever experiences in his life, and his whole lifetime is taken up in perfecting his adaptation to it, in striving to protect himself in that world and to squeeze out of it whatever gratification he can.

Strategies for Survival

It is in terms of these two cardinal characteristics of lower class life — poverty and a potentially destructive community — that lower class individuals work out their strategies for living.

In most of American society two grand strategies seem to attract the allegiance of its members and guide their day-to-day actions. These are the strategies of the good life and of career-success. A good-life strategy involves efforts to get along with others and not to rock the boat; it rests on a comfortable family environment with a stable vocation for husbands which enables them to be good providers. The strategy of career-success is the choice of ambitious men and women who see life as providing opportunities to move from a lower to a higher status, to "accomplish something," to achieve greater than ordinary material well-being, prestige, and social recognition. Both of these strategies are predicated on the assumption that the world is inherently rewarding if one behaves properly and does his part. The rewards of the world may come easily or only at the cost of great effort, but at least they are there for the individual who tries.

In slum worlds, little in the experience that individuals have as they grow up sustains a belief in a rewarding world. The strategies that seem appropriate are *strategies for survival*.

Three broad categories of lower class survival strategies can be observed. One is the strategy of the *expressive life style*. In response to the fact that the individual derives little security and reward from his membership in a family which can provide for and protect him, or from his experiences in the institutions in which he is expected to achieve (the school, later the job), individuals develop an exploitative strategy toward others. This strategy seeks to elicit rewards by making oneself interesting and attractive. In its benign forms, the expressive style is what attracts so many middle class people to the lower class — the fun, the singing, the dancing, the lively slang, the spontaneous gratification of impulse. But underneath the apparent spontaneity, the expressive style of lower class people is deadly serious business. It is by virtue of their ability to manipulate others by making themselves interesting and dramatic that the individual has an opportunity to get some of the few rewards that are available to him — whether these be gifts of money, a gambling bet won, the affections of a girl, or the right to participate in a community of peers, to drink with them, bum around with them, gain status in their eyes.

The individual learns by his expressive ability to "work game" on his peers, to "sound" on them, to "put them in a trick" (thereby raising his status by lowering the other fellow's). While the expressive style is central to preserving the stability and sanity of many (particularly younger) members of the lower class, the pursuit of expressive and self-dramatizing goals often results in behavior which makes trouble for the individual both from his own community and from representatives of conventional society. Dope addiction, drunkenness, illegitimacy, "spend-thrift behavior,' lack of interest in school on the part of adolescents — all can arise in part as a result of commitment to a strategy of "cool." For example, in Pruitt-Igoe teen-age boys drink and some smoke marijuana, in order to be able to loosen up enough to develop a "strong game" (i.e., a really persuasive line with peers or girls).

When the expressive strategy fails — because the individual cannot develop the required skills or because the audience is unappreciative — there is a great temptation to adopt a *violent strategy* in which you force others to give you what you need. The violent strategy is not a very popular one among lower class people. There is little really cold-blooded violence either toward persons or property in the slum world; most of it is undertaken out of a sense of desperation, a sense of deep insult to the self. Yet this strategy does not seem as distant and impossible to them as it does to the most prosperous.

Finally, there is the *depressive strategy* in which goals are increasingly constricted to the bare necessities for survival (not as a social being, but simply as an organism). This is the strategy of "I don't bother anybody and I hope nobody's gonna bother me; I'm simply going through the motions of keeping body (but not soul) together." Apparently this strategy of retreat and self-isolation is one that is adopted by more and more lower class men and women as they grow older, as the pay-offs from more expressive strategies begin to decline.

Hopes and Aspirations

And along with these strategies, lower class people make efforts to move in the direction of the more conventional strategies of the good life or (occasionally) of career-success. One can observe in the lives of individual families (or in whole groups, during times of extraordinary demand for lower class labor) a gradual shift away from the more destructive components of these survival strategies. It is from observations such as these, as well as from interviews about lower class people's hopes and aspirations, that one learns that lower class styles of life are pursued, not because they are received as intrinsically desirable, but because the people involved feel constrained to act in those ways given the deprivations and threats to which they find themselves subject. *The lower class does not have a separate system of basic values. Lower class people do not really "reject middle class values." It is simply that their whole experience of life teaches them that it is impossible to achieve a viable sense of self-esteem in terms of those values.*

But lower class people are also intimately alive to how things might be different. They know what they would like if only they had the resources of the average working class man — they would want a quiet, rather "square" life in a quiet neighborhood far from the dangers, seductions, and insults of the world in which they live. In the slums, there is no personal preference for — or sociological value attached to — matrifocal families, or a high incidence of premarital sexual relations resulting in unwanted pregnancies, or living alone as a deserted or divorced wife and having a boyfriend because you're afraid that if you remarry your welfare will be cut off or your new husband will not prove a stable provider. Lower class people are not easily confused how they must live and how they would like to live. What they might wish to preserve from the expressive heritage of lower class ways (particularly when, as among Negroes, those ways provide a kind of ethnic identity and not just a class identity) they feel that they can preserve while living a more stable kind of life. Lower class people would not find it nearly as agonizing as some intellectuals seem to feel they would to try to reconcile their traditions and their aspirations.

The Kenwood-Oakland Area, Chicago, Illinois*

"When a community changes from white to black, city officials lose interest in it, except for law and order."—State Representative Robert Mann, Chicago.

---

* U.S. Senate Select Committee on Nutrition and Human Needs, November 1969.

The streets of the Kenwood-Oakland community are an un-forgettable profile of destitution and deprivation. On every block, children play on crumbling sidewalks, amid rotting garbage and trash—much of it thrown there by commercial trash companies—and in condemned apartment houses with broken sewers.

Fifty thousand or more people, 85 percent Black are packed into the tenements lining the streets in the two square miles of the community. At least two people live in almost every room often, two or three to a bed. "One family moves into a small apartment in the area, then they are joined by another family, and another," says Dr. Joyce Lashof, Director of Community Medicine at Presbyterian-St. Luke's Hospital.

About half of the tenements are substandard. Many have no hot water, no air conditioning for the summer, no heat for the winter, poor lighting, falling plaster, peeling paint, roaches and rats.

Residents reportedly live here largely because they are faced with racial discrimination in real estate in other parts of the city. "You can't always prove there is discrimination," one woman said, "but you can tell by seeing how few black faces are permitted to live in the Federal housing projects for families with low incomes."

Each apartment costs more that $100 a month, although the average monthly rent in other parts of the city is $88. "This neighborhood, like other Black, urban areas, is the biggest gold mine since the California goldrush," one doctor said. Residents estimate that they pay a "color tax" of $20 a month to live in Kenwood-Oakland. Yet residents have less space, and much of it is substandard.

There is no library or park in the entire Kenwood-Oakland area. "The schools here are rotten," one child said. More than half of the residents have not finished high school. One elementary school had every single window broken and replaced by plywood sheets. No natural daylight entered the building. Indeed, sun barely penetrates into the dank, dark apartments or into the lives of the countless children living in Kenwood-Oakland. Recreation is in the alleys, the streets, the occasional fields of rubble where buildings once stood. The tour crossed one such "urban park," where perhaps 20 small children were playing in and around a rusting, abandoned car. This is their "playground."

Most of the children growing up in this environment are hungry. If their families depend on welfare, high rents consume most of the monthly budget. For at least 54,000 hungry Chicago families, food becomes a second priority. "At the end of the month, our children usually survive on candy bars," one woman told us. "After all, it is energy food and cheap."

Most food is not cheap, and most of it is inferior. We walked through a major grocery store and saw moldy melons, grossly discolored meat, overpriced and fatigued vegetables. Missing were foods familiar to Black people, but tempting were costly frozen desserts, for which few in the community have home freezers, and a shining liquor display as you enter the store. A study of the Senate Select Committee on Malnutrition and Hunger revealed at least 54,000 hungry Chicago families. "Hunger is not a hurting thing. It is a halting force with respect to the progress of a nation toward goals of unity, cohesion, and growth," stated Reverend Jesse Jackson of Operation Breadbasket.

Depression and despair greeted us in each house we visited. We spoke to a woman whose apartment just recently had been condemned by city officials. She had to relocate herself and her seven children within four weeks. She had no place to go nor any idea how to seek housing she could afford. "But I guess anything will be better than living here," she said. Each time she goes to sleep, she fears fire. There have been numerous fires in her building because of poor wiring. "There is no janitor to keep drunks and other riff-raff out of the empty rooms here. The doors won't lock and there is nothing here but women and children." When it rains, she said, everything gets wet because the roof leaks. "And it doesn't just leak in certain places where it could be caught with pans. It leaks all over. Even my beds get wet." Reeking sewage was backed up in her toilet. She showed how she flushed the waste with a hose from the sink to the toilet.

"It's not as bad now as it was last winter," she said. "Then I had to even go without water for two weeks." On some winter days, there is no heat.

One of her neighbors also told of plumbing problems. "My children can't flush toilets or take baths," she said. The toilet, located just next to her apartment for the use of several families, floods daily. She has attached a hose leading from the toilet to a nearby sink to prevent flooding, but water still overflows.

This tiny, extremely nervous lady also described her attempts to get care for her 2-year-old child who weighs only 23 pounds and is frequently feverish. "I just don't know what to do for him. I keep taking him to the doctors, but they can't find out what's wrong." She and her five children reside in a four-room apartment filled with the stench of uncollected garbage. She pays $100 a month in rent. We noted that her baby had passed one of Kenwood-Oakland's most critical tests—living past his second week. About 45 of every 1,000 babies born in Kenwood-Oakland die in early infancy, it was reported.

Another woman told of being unable to have a colostomy repaired because she could not repay 11 pints of blood she had received during a previous operation. The supervisor of the Cook County Hospital's blood bank explained that patients are normally asked to repay blood before being given any additional surgery, except during an emergency.

One lady told how she watched her baby die while waiting three hours for care in an emergency room at Cook County Hospital. "They expect you to wait hours for emergency care there." Most of the Black residents of Chicago, however, still use this hospital. Black people occupy 85 per cent of the beds there.

The hospital's clinic handles more than two-thirds of the outpatient care for the city's Black citizens. Why do the Blacks go there? A recent University of Chicago survey revealed that Blacks continue to depend on Cook County Hospital because it is the one institution where they know they will not be refused care—if they can tolerate the time to travel there and wait for service. A more pressing reason is the paucity of physicians in Chicago's Black ghettos. There were five physicians for the

50,000 or more residents of Kenwood-Oakland until the community itself closed down the business of a pair of unsanitary, disreputable doctors.

"We can't be expected to bus white doctors into the city by day and send them home by night," explained Doctor Risher Watts, who represents the Cook County Physicians Association. "We need to train more Negro physicians to serve the people of the inner city. Even more important is learning how to keep the few physicians we have now." He said that the few specialists who had practiced near Kenwood-Oakland moved away because they could not be assured prompt and full payment by the State for the many welfare patients they were expected to treat. "Rather than fight the system, they just moved out." Consequently, as Pierre DeVise, DePauw University urbanologist, concluded: "We have very separate and unequal facilities and services that pass for health care."

Who is to blame in this degradation of life and health? Is it the penalty of being poor or being Black? Or both? "I think in the list of active enemies of health in this community, we have already identified, first, the political structure and City Hall," stated a community practitioner. "Second, we have to identify organized medicine, with its platitudes, and third, the health care system, which is guaranteed to make shortages by rewarding those who go to the affluent parts of the system instead of into places of grave need."

In an effort to achieve a health care system responsive to the needs of the local communities, the residents of Chicago in 1966 voted for a $5 million dollar bond issue to be used in conjunction with Federal grants to build 10 neighborhood health centers. The bonds have been floated, but the city has so far refused to release the money. Two neighborhood centers have been built, but solely with Federal money. Most residents are pessimistic that the City will release the funds in the near future. "The people have spoken, but who are the people?" one resident asked.

If someone had decided to design a system to break people's spirit, and to break them as human beings, they couldn't have done a better job.

Chapter Six

RACE

There are many inequities in our American society, but none more troublesome, wrong, and unnecessary than those directly related to race. Minorities have nearly always suffered at the hands of the majorities—the problems are not new. We believe it is time that Americans realize and practice what the Constitution of the United States clearly sets forth—that we are all, regardless of race, religion, sex, or national origin, full-fledged citizens and entitled to equal consideration under our laws. Certainly one can question the need for the Civil Rights Legislation of the 50's and 60's if our people had in fact fully supported the Constitution as written.

We are all too familiar with the statistics of the Mexican–American, the Indians, and the Negro. His life expectancy is lower; he is short-changed in education, employment opportunities, decent housing, pay, types of work, and medical care. The Negro child, in particular, is further handicapped: one–third of those under 14 live in homes where at least one parent is missing. The missing male leads to female dominance of the family. The morale of the male is further lowered by problems of employment and occupational status. This situation must be reversed if the social structure of the Negro is to be changed.

The American Indian has been treated shabbily since the coming of the white man. He lost his land and his hunting grounds as he was relentlessly pursued and forced onto the reservations. He was given handouts; minimum funds and care were provided, just enough to keep him below the threshold of revolt. He was not even considered human, and only recently has he gained the status of citizenship. The Indian, like the Negro, has been deprived of an opportunity for education and the resultant qualifications for employment. Both grow more militant as they demand that they be granted their due: full rights of citizenship and the advantages accruing therefrom.

Perhaps the most important thing that has happened in our land is the determined effort being made by our deprived minorities to gain a share of the "good life." If our nation is to grow and prosper then our minorities must be a meaningful part of the process; otherwise divisive efforts will cause our nation to explode into nightmare.

The Negro and Deprivation*

Family Structure and Employment Problems

Harold L. Sheppard and Herbert E. Striner

This report places strong emphasis upon the relationship of family structure and size to the problems of employment and job status for many Negroes. At the outset, it should be stressed that there is no such thing as *the* Negro family and that there is nothing intrinsically pathological about different family structures or sizes. Because of the great lack of research and data concerning the relationship of family structure and size to employment and economic opportunity, much of what follows is necessarily inferential. There is great need for gathering data explicitly for the purpose of more systematic research on this

---

* *Civil Rights, Employment, and the Social Status of American Negroes*, published by the W. E. Upjohn Institute for Employment Research, June 1966.

subject. Recent discussions of this topic have tended to engender acrimonious debate instead of needed research. Unless a calmer, more empirical analysis is undertaken, a solution to the employment problems of Negroes will not be found.

The large-scale migration of Negroes during the forties and fifties has had a profound effect on their families. This impact on the families is heaped upon repercussions from the plantation and slavery system. In any evaluation of differences between the Negro family and the white family, it is quickly apparent that the former is much more frequently identified with the poverty but an even closer look is required. Nonwhite poverty families have, on the average, more children than white poverty families. There is a direct relationship between a large number of children in a family and frustrating experience; and this correlation provides a pessimism base, an unconscious or conscious disposition to believe that "we just can't beat the game." The problem of planning family size, unfortunately, is being faced very late. But it is being faced at last; and the issue of employment and economic security cannot be divorced from the outcome of present and future family planning programs.

The following table presents the comparative distribution of large size families among whites and Negroes, and the relationship of size to poverty:

Table 1. Distribution of Negro and White Families in Poverty, by Number of Children Under 18, 1963

All families with children under 18 (percent)	Families with 1 child (percent)		Families with 6 or more children (percent)	
	Negro	White	Negro	White
22	33	10	77	35

NOTE. — Based on the less rigorous "economy" level criteria established by the Social Security Administration (Mollie Orshansky, "Counting the Poor: Another Look at the Poverty Profile," *Social Security Bulletin,* January 1965).

Such comparisons show that the larger the family the greater the poverty. Furthermore, there is a greater proportion of larger families among Negroes than among whites. *Given the continuing differential in birth rates between poor whites and Negros, it is possible for the problem to become even more acute among Negroes.* As Philip Hauser has pointed out, "The Negro, like the inhabitant of the developing regions in Asia, Latin America, and Africa, in his new exposure to amenities of twentieth-century living, is experiencing rapidly declining mortality while fertility rates either remain high or, as in urban areas, actually increase."[1]

Furthermore, for every 100 Negroes between the ages of 20 and 64 in 1960, there were 94 under 20, while the corresponding ratios for whites in the same year was only 75. In other words, Negroes of working ages carry a greater burden of dependency than whites. As of 1965, there were 103 Negroes under 20 for every 100 aged 20-64.

In 1960, one-third of all nonwhite children under the age of 14—as contrasted to only one-twelfth of white children in the same age group—were living and being reared in the absence of one or both parents, usually the absence of the father. About 20 percent of all nonwhite children were living with mothers only, as contrasted with less than 6 percent of white children. There are no data on how many Negroes have lived in fatherless families during all of their childhood. Living in a fatherless family is especially difficult for boys in their developmental years. The emergence of this type of pattern as an urban phenomenon is suggested by the fact that, in 1965, 25.5 percent of nonfarm Negro families were headed by females, in contrast to only 15.3 percent among farm families, according to the Bureau of the Census.

With one-third of Negro children under 14 being reared in families with one or both parents absent, economic equality with whites for large numbers of Negroes (perhaps growing numbers) can only be a pious wish. There is nothing intrinsically

---

1. "Demographic Factors in the Integration of the Negro," *Daedalus* (Fall, 1965), 864.

immoral about fatherless or motherless family structures—
unless we view as immoral in our type of society and economy
high unemployment rates, low income, and exhausting occupations. Nor is there anything intrinsically immoral about matri-
archal families if there is an adequate role for the husband and
son to perform in such families and in the general society.

As long as there are large families in low-income, low-
skilled, poorly schooled populations—white or Negro—we must
strive to design more effective means of attaining progress in
income and occupational status. Low-income rural-origin families with large numbers of children have a high rate of dropouts. And dropouts have a higher unemployment rate than high
school graduates. Thus, there seems to be a definite correlation
between birth in a large low-income, rural-origin family and
low job status and high unemployment. In other words, the
nature and size of the family can become a condition for poor
jobs and unemployment. Generally speaking, birth rates actually
have declined in periods of unemployment in our history; that
is, extended unemployment has tended to be followed by declines
in birth rates. It would be interesting, incidentally, to trace
historically white-Negro differences, if any, in birth rate "ad-
justments" to changes in nonfarm unemployment rates.

The fact that in urban centers Negroes currently have a
higher proportion of low-income recent migrant persons and
larger families than whites creates the impression of a "Negro
problem." Many Negroes become sensitive to such a description.
Many whites use the description as a defense against any action
that would change such a fact, thus indulging in a self-fulfilling
prophecy. It may also be possible that some Negro leaders, by
refusing to cope with these facts, are also participating in self-
fulfilling of the prophecy.

In years past, we witnessed the reluctance on the part of
whites and Negroes alike to accept the proposition that education is a crucial variable in the life chances of Negroes. Prej-
udiced whites insisted that biology was the sole underlying
cause of Negro inequality, while many Negroes insisted that
discrimination was the sole cause. Biology certainly was not
and is not the explanation, but discrimination on the basis of

skin color alone is no longer as crucial as it was in the past (although it is far from being eradicated). The main point, however, is that Negroes and whites now accept the importance of educational improvements as one of the means or conditions for equality.

Since education and training are recognized today as making a difference between success and failure in the world of work, it has become almost trite and platitudinous to state that Negroes must be given better and more education and training. What has not been recognized sufficiently is that one—and *only one* —of the obstacles to rapid progress toward this goal for more Negroes is the nature of the family structure in a significant minority of the Negro population in urban areas. This minority has a greater birth rate, and it may thus be on the way to becoming a larger minority than before—*the result of which can be a perpetuation of the very crisis we are trying to prevent or mitigate.* One statistical aspect of this differential birth rate is that 64 percent of all the nonfarm, nonwhite poor population living in families are 21 years of age or younger—a proportion 21 percent higher than that among white poor persons living in nonfarm families. Among the nonwhites who are not poor, about one-half were 21 or younger.

The modern American urban world encompasses a caste system that has emerged out of the migrations of the descendants of 19th century slavery. As St. Clair Drake has pointed out:

> ... the character of the Black Ghetto is not set by the newer "gilded," not-yet run down portions of it, but by the older sections where unemployment rates are high and the masses of people work with their hands—where the median level of education is just above graduation from grade school and many of the people are likely to be recent migrants from rural areas.

> The "ghettoization" of the Negro has resulted in the emergence of a ghetto subculture with a distinctive ethos, most pronounced, perhaps, in Harlem, but recognizable in all Negro neighborhoods. . . . The spontaneous vigor of the children who crowd streets and playgrounds ... and the cheerful

rushing about of adults, free from the occupational pressures
of the "white world" in which they work, create an atmosphere
of warmth and superficial intimacy which obscures the unpleasant facts of life in the overcrowded rooms behind the
doors, the lack of adequate maintenance standards, and the
too prevalent vermin and rats.[2]

About 60 percent of Negro families in the United States earn
less than $4,000 per year, while 60 percent of white families
earn more than that amount. Within the Negro low-income segment there is naturally a heterogeneity of social strata and
styles of life. Many low-income Negroes behave within a system
of what has come to be called "middle class" values, including
a stress on respectability and decorum; getting an education
(if not for themselves, at least for their children) ; family stability; and a reasonable family size. To quote Drake, "For both
men and women, owning a home and going into business are
highly desired goals, the former being a realistic one, the latter
a mere fantasy."[3]

But within this same income category there are other types
of families and individuals. This part of the urban Negro population and its style of life provide the flesh-and-blood world
from which spring the statistics of the "Moynihan" Report:

> ... an "unorganized" lower class exists whose members
> tend always to become disorganized—functioning in an anomic
> situation where gambling, excessive drinking, the use of nar-
> cotics, and sexual promiscuity are prevalent forms of behavior,
> and violent interpersonal relations reflect an ethos of suspicion
> and resentment which suffuses this deviant subculture. It is
> within this milieu that criminal and semi-criminal activities
> burgeon.[4]

The maintenance of a middle class style of life requires more
than sheer perseverance and will power. It also calls for a cer-

2. "The Social and Economic Status of the Negro in the United States,"
   Daedalus (Fall 1965), 771-772.
3. *Ibid.*, 779.
4. *Loc. cit.*

tain level of income (more precisely, a certain level of purchasing power) and perhaps even a certain kind of family structure. Purchasing power is not distributed and occupational and family structure are not organized among Negroes to the same degree as they are among whites. The issue is, can one be changed without changing the others?

In this respect, a vicious circle continued to pervade the social world of many Negroes in which the number of families without fathers and a lower prestige of males among their female associates and their children are dominant features. The pattern of Negro male insecurity, sustained by other current conditions, continues to be a major obstacle in effectuating a distinct break from the disadvantaged position of a large part of the Negro population today. For one thing, "An impressive body of evidence indicates that rather serious personality distortions result from the female dominance so prevalent in the Negro subculture. . . ."[5] What is not sufficiently recognized is the link between the nature of the social status of many Negro males today and their problems of employment and occupational status. Indeed, this link is often vehemently denied.

The low esteem of the Negro male, especially in the lower income strata, must be given prime attention in any serious effort to change the social structure of American Negro society which is much more like a pyramid than the white social structure. Negro occupational structure, for example, consists of a miniscule capstone of upper class families, a larger stratum of middle class families under that, and the largest class at the bottom. Conversely, white social structure is shaped more like a diamond, with a large middle class bulge.

This situation of a large number of Negro males warrants further comment. For example, Negro boys in lower income families receive less and even inferior education compared to Negro girls. Smaller proportions enroll in college-preparatory and commercial classes in the high schools. Even if the girls in such classes do not actually enter college, they at least become more qualified for white-collar jobs—the occupational sector

5. *Ibid.*, 787.

which is expanding at a greater rate than manual jobs. As one study has pointed out:

> When more white-collar occupations open up for Negroes, the girls will be better prepared and more motivated to fill them than the boys. This is true for clerical and sales positions, but also for semi-professional and professional ones. Under these conditions Negro girls, especially those of a working class background, can be expected to achieve higher occupational status than the boys from their socio-economic category. This kind of development would tend to perpetuate the highest prestige position of Negro women with the Negro group.[6]

The author of that study also confirms one of the major theses of this bulletin, namely, that the disadvantaged position of Negroes can persist even when discrimination itself declines or is actually eliminated, especially in the case of Negro males. If this is so, the civil rights movement and the drive for equal job status face some severe frustrations. Unless major changes can be brought about in the demography, sociology, and psychology of lower income Negro families, and of males in particular, civil rights legislation for fair employment practices will not soon achieve its goal. At best, the only kinds of jobs available for unskilled Negro males born and reared in such family settings are actually declining, and the large numbers involved cannot possibly be absorbed.

The adverse character of families in substantial parts of the Negro population is certainly due in large part to (1) the heritage of past decades and (2) the nature of their present environmental setting. In other words, it may be looked upon as an effect, a result. But effects can assume a causative role in human affairs.[7] Illegitimacy, many children in a family, and

6. Jetse Sprey, "Sex Differences in Occupational Choice Patterns among Negro Adolescents," *Social Problems* (*Summer*, 1962), 22.

7. The family problem does exist and also does affect efforts to move the Negro into the economy and the society on a comparable footing with the white. But to be really effective, one must see the family factor not as the sole or major focus of our efforts, but as one of many crucial focuses. We are faced with a social simultaneous equation where the solution can only result if all factors are dealt with in the solving process.

unstable parental relations have their effects, too; they should not be looked upon merely as results of other factors if we intend to deal with the problem and not just continue to look for someone or something to blame.

A large number of children is obviously an insuperable burden for a low-income family, regardless of racial background. In this particular instance, just on the aggregate level, the average income of Negro families is about 50 percent of the average income of white families, but the average number of children in Negro families is 30 percent more than in white families. Putting it even more dramatically, while the average number of children in upper income nonwhite families has fallen below that of whites with comparable economic characteristics, the average number of children for lower income nonwhites is above that for comparable whites. According to the 1960 Census, for every 1,000 nonwhite females aged 15-19 who had ever been married, 1,247 children had been born unto them. For comparable white females, the corresponding figure was 725.

The basic point that the growth in the Negro population is concentrated among those with low income, inadequate education, employment insecurity, and unstable family structure.

If we are sincere in our statements about the crisis nature of Negro income, employment, and occupational status, it is not enough to be comforted by long-run predictions that, like others before them, Negroes will decrease their rural exodus to urban areas and thus eventually produce a population "increasingly similar to others in the areas to which they have come."[8] For one thing, there is nothing inevitable about such a prediction. Even if it were inevitable, the current rate of change is actually so slow that it could take more than 100 years to reach "parity." Certainly, recent trends in income and occupational status do not point to any optimistic conclusion about the future.

Hauser points to the impact of the higher birth rate among Negroes on their socioeconomic status:

---

8. Hauser, *Daedalus* (Fall, 1965), 865.

High fertility with its consequent large family size handicaps the Negro by limiting the investment the family can make in human resources—that is, in the education and training of the child. Under economic pressure the Negro child, on the one hand, has little incentive to remain in school and, on the other, is often forced to leave even when he desires to obtain an education. Thus, the Negro child tends to be the high school drop-out rather than the high school graduate. Even if much more is done to remove the Negro family from the bitter consequences of raw poverty, large numbers of children will tend to set limits on the education each child in the Negro community will receive. Certainly, the family with two or three children will, for some time to come, be in a better position to support its children through high school than the family with six or more children.

The poverty of the Negro family must rank as the single most important factor preventing the Negro from developing those abilities which could help him to assume both the rights and obligations of being a first-class American citizen ... the large proportion of Negro children now under eighteen cannot possibly be expected to participate fully in the mainstream of American life so long as they are steeped in the morass of poverty.[9]

Since education is becoming a much more important requirement for eliminating Negro-white economic differentials and for increasing job opportunities, and since "large numbers of children will tend to set limits on the education each child in the Negro community will receive," we must come face to face with the subject of family structure and size. This matter is more than a spurious factor in the issue of Negro progress in employment and occupational status. To put it more directly by quoting Hauser, "As a result of a high birth rate, the Negro population retains characteristics such as inferior occupations, low income, and a style of life precluding association and social interaction

9. *Ibid.*, 865-866.

with the dominant white society—all of which retard assimilation."[10] This statement underscores the authors' view that a high birth rate among low-income families can itself serve to perpetuate inferior occupations and high unemployment rates.

The vicious circle of poverty, large family size, poor education and skills, and high unemployment rates must be broken. It *can* be broken. And a vicious circle can be entered and broken at many points of its circumference. One of these points of entry relates to family size. We need a massive effective program aimed at helping "the relatively uneducated and impoverished Negro family to restrict its size." If all Negroes were in the upper 5 percent of the income distribution, concern about family size would, of course, be irrelevant (or indicative of fears of Negro dominance). Millionaires—Negro or white—can afford to have families of six or more children. The only adverse effect would be smaller inheritances for each child. Low-income persons—Negro or white—cannot afford large families, at least in the current stage of human history.

Poverty, poor education, punitive welfare policies (such as the "man-in-the-house" rule), and even pathological discrimination, have all contributed to the economic and social-psychological frustrations of our Negro citizens. Such frustrations are a result of these and other patterns created and sustained by dominant white beliefs and practices. But again, results can, in turn, become causes. Today, the inferior role and status of low-income Negro males contribute to the perpetuation of Negro inequality in general. "There is a great need for special efforts to enhance the role of the Negro male in the family, to concentrate on providing him with the capabilities of taking on his expected functions, responsibilities, and obligations as husband, father, and provider."[11] These capabilities also depend on the less understood, but nevertheless real, pschological phenomena such as self-identity, ego strength, etc. These factors are among the causes, as well as among the effects, of the employment problem.

---

10. *Ibid.*, 866.

11. *Ibid.*, 867.

The psychological literature is replete with findings about the unique personality problems of Negro males from lower income families. Department of Labor and Bureau of the Census data on economic and demographic characteristics offer only partial—and hence inadequate—information and "explanations" about the employment problem of Negroes. Furthermore, the data too frequently understate the problem by being reported in the category of nonwhites instead of Negroes specifically and exclusively.

The research findings on Negro males in particular, as well as on the impact of fatherless situations on basic behavior patterns and motivations, have been summarized by Thomas Pettigrew. One of his passages supports the authors' position that the employment problems of Negroes (males in particular) cannot be separated from family structure.

> ... eight-and-nine-year-old children whose fathers are absent seek immediate gratification far more than children whose fathers are present in the home. For example, when offered their choice of receiving a tiny candy bar immediately or a large bar a week later, fatherless children typically take the small bar while other children prefer to wait for the larger bar. This hunger for immediate gratification among fatherless children seems to have serious implications. Regardless of race, children manifesting this trait also tend to be less accurate in judging time, less "socially responsible," less oriented toward achievement and more prone to delinquency. Indeed, two psychologists maintain that the inability to delay gratification is a critical factor in immature, criminal, and neurotic behavior.

> ... Various studies have demonstrated the crucial importance of the father in the socialization of boys. Mothers raising their children in homes without fathers are frequently overprotective, sometimes even smothering, in their compensatory attempts to be a combined father and mother . . . boys whose fathers are not present have initially identified with their mothers and must later, in America's relatively patrifocal society, develop a conflicting, secondary identification with males . . .

Several studies point to the applicability of this sex-identity problem to lower-class Negro males.[12]

Lower income Negroes have experienced difficulty in the learning process, as Martin Deutsch pointed out.[13] He also described how the economic and social experiences of the low-income Negro male have influenced his "concept of himself and his general motivation to succeed in competitive areas of society where the rewards are the greatest. . . . the lower-class Negro child entering school often has had no experience with a 'successful' male model or thereby with a psychological framework in which effort can result in at least the possibility of achievement. . . . A child from any circumstance who has been deprived of a substantial portion of the variety of stimuli which he is maturationally capable of responding to is likely to be deficient in the equipment required for learning." Deutsch and Brown have also shown that even when income is held constant, the IQ's of Negro pupils from families without a father present are lower than the IQ's of those from families with a father.[14]

The large urban areas of the United States are fostering and are subject to a set of adverse social conditions affecting young Negroes — especially the males. These boys are too frequently in fatherless and/or unemployed families; they lack adequate stimulation for achievement, adequate occupational guidance (often nonexistent) in the families and the schools and sufficient occupational training; and they obtain only blind-end jobs, if any. The "choice" of a first job is itself a vital variable; an unskilled (or nonskilled) worker typically takes the only job he knows about when entering the labor market,

---

12. *A Profile of the Negro American* (Princeton: Van Nostrand, 1964), pp. 17-19.

13. "The Disadvantaged Child and the Learning Process," *in* A. H. Passow, ed., *Education in Depressed Areas* (New York: Teachers College, Columbia University, 1963, pp. 163-179.

14. Martin Deutsch and Bert Brown, "Social Influences in Negro-White Intelligence Differences," *Social Issues* (April, 1964), 28.

and this job is stigmatized by a low wage and/or frequent spells of layoffs. If young Negroes are not poorly motivated to begin with, they inevitably lower their aspirations and efforts at self-improvement as a result of the syndrome of environmental insults. Even the pernicious system of easy credit and exorbitant interest operates to discourage their active jobseeking once unemployed, since their income from jobs would only be garnisheed by their creditors. The unemployed have their own version of cost-benefit analysis too.

David McClelland, of Harvard University, who has studied extensively the role of motivation in economic behavior, has pointed out that the conditions of slavery influenced the nature of American Negro adjustment conducive to obedience but not to achievement and self-betterment; and that it should not be surprising to find that many of the descendants of slavery—even though "free"—still show the effects of such adjustment. It is significant that for those few Negroes who have become middle and upper class, their achievement motivation (as measured by McClelland's projective test approach) is conspicuously high—"reflecting once again the fact that individuals who have managed to move out of a low . . . achievement [motivation] group tend to have exceptionally high motivation."[15]

The relevance of the family structure to the individual's motivations to succeed—to aspire to and obtain better jobs, more education, and training — should be made clear to persons concerned with the job and income status of Negroes. A number of studies have indicated that people whose fathers were absent during their childhood tend not to develop such motivations.[16] Neither Negroes nor the nation as a whole will benefit if we create the conditions for greater opportunities in employment without preparing Negroes to take actual advantage of these conditions and opportunities. Part of this preparation

---

15. *The Achieving Society* (Princeton: Van Nostrand, 1961), p. 377.

16. For example, W. Mischel, "Father-Absence and Delay of Gratification," *Journal of Abnormal and Social Psychology*, Liii (1961),, 116-125; R. L. Nuttall, "Some Correlates of High Need for Achievement among Urban Northern Negroes," *Journal of Abnormal and Social Psychology*, LViii (1964, 593-600.

must include a full-scale program of restructuring the motivational conditions of Negroes, again especially Negro males. This
attack must enlist the active leadership of Negroes themselves,
with the financial and organizational support from public and
private sources. Some Negro leaders have already taken the
initiative in the formulation of part of the issue in these terms,
notably Whitney Young, Jr., of the Urban League. Since he has
professional background in the field of social work and community organization, this is to be expected. We must, however, per-
suade others that these considerations are involved in the economic problems of Negroes, not merely as effects but as causes.

In a 1963 study, in Philadelphia,[17] it was found that lower
status Negro mothers had lower educational and job aspirations
for their sons than did higher status Negro mothers; they were
less certain about aspirations for their sons than for their
daughters (which was not true of higher status mothers). Compared to higher status mothers, a much higher percentage of
these mothers said that 21 years of age or under is the best
age for their sons to marry and 19 years of age for their daughters. This finding is crucial because "if a mother holds high educational and occupational aspirations for her children and at
the same time thinks they should marry young and have a large
family, there is often, by implication, a contradiction in her aspirations." And the younger the age at marriage, the greater
the chances for bearing more children. If one keeps in mind
the high percentage of mother-dominated families (even in
families where the father is present) in Negro urban lower income groups, these findings have a significant bearing on the
occupational and employment progress of Negro males. Given
the importance of the mother in Negro lower income urban families, her aspirations can adversely influence the future of her
offspring—even in the face of rising job opportunities as a
result of economic growth and fair employment legislation.

      ... the relative positions of Negro mothers in the lower

_____

17. Robert R. Bell, "Lower Class Negro Mothers' Aspirations for their
    Children," *Social Forces*, (May, 1965), 493-500.

class may be related to different aspirational values transmitted to their children, and may also contribute to a way of life which makes any alternative aspirational levels difficult for their children to internalize and possibly achieve.[18]

If such lower aspirations operate at the lower end of the lower income group's values system, the greater is the need for agencies and institutions to exercise a positive role in reshaping the goals of Negro youths who lack such motivation. The schools, training programs, the employment service, OEO, and other agencies in the community have much to do. If they fail, the less likely will it be that values conducive to occupational upgrading can be injected into the thinking and behavior of these groups of Negroes, especially the males. Negro adults must not be excluded from such attention, either.

Much of this reshaping must be carried out by the larger society, too. Once opportunities are available, the larger society and the government in general cannot simply stand aside and watch. What whites do in addition will also play a role in the motivational environment of Negroes. What motivation is there for a young Negro to graduate from high school when he sees that whites with high school diplomas earn one-third more than Negroes with similar schooling? How can a young Negro aspire to enter an apprenticeship program when he might be required to serve for four to seven years before he enjoys the fruits of such training? How can a young Negro adult with a family to support enter a training program, instead of taking a job as a laborer, for 16 to 52 weeks if the training is less than the immediate income as a common laborer, and if the job for which he may be trained seems to be a dead-end one?

The responsibility for helping low-motivated Negroes to improve themselves lies partly in community institutions such as the schools. But the teachers are not yet equipped with the appropriate techniques to perform this task. Any program aimed at raising the motivations and aspirations of those Negro youths who are frustrated, and who often have ample reason

18. *Ibid.*, 500.

for frustration, will in and of itself be a motivating factor in
their lives. If someone pays attention to them and is sincerely
concerned about their future, a large number of them will respond favorably. There is a great urgency for a vast program
to train large numbers of Negro male "motivators" to serve in
this role.[19]

The Angry American Indian:
Starting Down the Protest Trail Time*

Most Americans know the first Americans only by cliché.
There is the 19th century image, caught in bronze and in litho-
graph, of the defeated warrior, head drooping forward so that
his feathers nearly mingle with his pony's mane. The bow of his
shoulders and the slump of his body evoke his loss of pride, of
green and fertile lands, of earth's most favored continent. Then
there is a recent image, often seen through air-conditioned au-
tomobile windows. Grinning shyly, the fat squaw hawks her
woven baskets along the reservation highway, the dusty land-
scape littered with rusting cars, crumbling wickiups and bony
cattle. In the bleak villages, the only signs of cheer are romping,
round-faced children and the invariably dirty, crowded bar,
noisy with the shouts and laughter of drunkenness.

Like most stereotypes, these caricatures possess a certain

---

19. In this connection, David McClelland now believes that he and his asso-
    ciates at Harvard (Sterling Livingston, George Litwin, and others) have
    techniques for increasing the achievement motivation of individuals. His
    proposals deserve serious consideration by public and private agencies
    concerned with the issue of employment progress among Negroes. See
    "Achievement Motivation Can Be Developed," *Harvard Business Review*,
    (November-December, 1965).

* Reprinted with permission from TIME, The Weekly Magazine; Copyright
  Time, Inc. 1970.

core of validity. They also help white America contain and numb the reality of past guilt and present injustice. Most important of all, they are less and less significant. After more than a century of patience and passivity, the nation's most neglected and isolated minority is astir, seeking the means and the muscle for protest and redress. Sometimes highly educated, sometimes speaking with an articulateness forged of desperation, always angry, the new American Indian is fed up with the destitution and publicly sanctioned abuse of his long-divided people. He is raising his voice and he intends to be heard. Listen:

"The next time whites try to illegally clear our land, perhaps we should get out and shoot the people in the bulldozers," contends Michael Benson, a 19-year-old Navajo and a freshman at Wesleyan University.

"It's time that Indians got off their goddam asses and stopped letting white people lead them around by their noses," says Lehman Brightman, a South Dakota Sioux now working on a Ph.D. at Berkeley. "Even the name Indian is not ours. It was given to us by some dumb honky who got lost and thought he'd landed in India."

"We weren't meant to be tourist attractions for the master race," scoffs Gerald Wilkinson, 30, a Cherokee who holds multiple degrees after attending four universities. "We don't use the language of the New Left, but that doesn't mean we're not militant."

"Some day you're going to feel like Custer, baby," shouted one unidentified Indian at Donald Dwyer, a former Minneapolis police chief recently invited to discuss city problems with a group of Minneapolis Indians.

Symbolic Protest

That kind of rhetoric is surprising, coming from people long accustomed to equating silence with dignity. But in acts as well as speech, the newly aroused Indian is no longer content to play the obsequious Tonto to the white man's Lone Ranger. A belligerent band of 100 Indians still occupies the abandoned federal prison at Alcatraz, which the Indians propose to use as a cul-

tural center and are willing to buy—for $24 in glass beads and
red cloth." Says one of the invaders: "Alcatraz is still better
than most reservations." Angered at the whites, who litter their
beaches with beer cans and broken bottles, Indians in the state
of Washington set up road blocks and closed 50 miles of sea-
shore. A group of 50 Passamaquoddy Indians in Maine charged
motorists fees to pass through their land on a busy highway
last July. Four Indians at Dartmouth College, which was
founded partly "for civilizing and christianizing Children of
Pagans," protested the Indian dress of the college mascot, and
officials banished it from football games.

Going beyond such symbolic acts, Indians in Washington
have deliberately violated fishing regulations that they consider
a breach of their rights, and have gone to jail as a result. One
of their leaders, Janet McCloud, a fiery Tutalip, contends that
restrictions on catching salmon have reduced the Indian to
"savages with no more rights than a bear." More softly, she
concedes: "I don't like being a clown or a militant, but sometimes you have to break this conspiracy of silence." Another
angry woman, Kahn Tineta Horn, effectively uses a trim figure
in a tight buckskin dress to gain television attention for protest
demonstrations. But sex is not her only weapon; she has been
arrested for carrying a knife and for interfering with police.

Harassment by police is the target of a sophisticated Indian
uprising in Minneapolis, which has one of the few Indian ghettos in any city. There Clyde Bellecourt, 33, a tough Chippewa
who has spent 14 years behind bars, has organized an "Indian
Patrol." Dressed in red jackets, its members use short-wave
radios to follow police activity, then show up to observe the
cops silently whenever an Indian gets into trouble. After the
patrol was formed, there were no arrests of Indians for 22
straight weekends. Ironically, it was during a prison term for
burglary that Bellecourt decided he could help other Indians. "I
read a lot of books," he says, "and I started finding out that I
wasn't a savage, that I wasn't dirty—and that I was smart."
For his work, he is paid a salary by the Urban Coalition.

The new Indian activism is gradually beating its way into

the nation's consciousness—and into its conscience. In ways
both salutary and shabby, Indians are becoming fashionable.
As The New Yorker's Calvin Trillin recently observed: *"It is
almost possible to hear the drums in the East Sixties."*

The Indian is spicing his protest with a grim kind of humor.
His slogans proclaim: KEMO SABE MEANS HONKY, RED POWER!
and CUSTER HAD IT COMING. More stingingly, Indian Folk Singer
Buffy Sainte-Marie, a Cree with a degree in education and Ori-
ental philosophy, confronts white audiences with pointed lyrics:

*When a war between nations is lost
The loser, we know, pays the cost;
But even when Germany fell to your hands
You left them their pride and you left them their land.*

The national abuse of the Indian reached Broadway last
year as the subject of serious drama. Arthur Kopit's *Indians*
played only twelve weeks; some critics considered it noisy, dis-
organized theater; some audiences seemed to find the penitential
message discomfiting. A pro-Indian movie, *Little Big Man,* star-
ring Dustin Hoffman, has been filmed on Montana's Crow reservation. It portrays George Custer as a villain leading troops
bent on genocide. Three books personalizing Indian alienation
have won critical acclaim. A novel, *House Made of Dawn,* by N.
Scott Momaday, a Kiowa who teaches English at Berkeley, won
a Pulitzer prize last year. *Custer Died for Your Sins,* by Vine
Deloria, a Standing Rock Sioux, wryly details the Indians' own
infighting and their frustrations in dealing with white society.
Our Brother's Keeper: The Indian in White America angrily
indicts whites for keeping the Indian a stranger in his home-
land—"America's prisoner of war."

On the fad level, a budding renaissance of Indian cultural
accouterments has inspired pot-smoking teen-agers and high-
fashion socialites to don beaded necklaces, fringed jackets, Indian belts, bikinis and feathers. Most Indians scoff at the af-
fectation and claim that much of the clothing is foreign made.

The Handicap of Dignity

Why has it taken the Indian so long to rouse himself to turn his ire toward action? Many a white bureaucrat, ruling a reservation like a colonial army officer, has assumed that Indian acquiescence stemmed from either respect or servility. Rarely has it been either. The Indian nation was physically shattered and spiritually demoralized by the U.S. Cavalry, which systematically destroyed its leaders and the best of its manhood in the late 19th century campaigns that whites euphemistically call the pacification of the West. Long before the white man's arrival, Indian tribes had, of course, waged limited war upon one another over hunting rights, and raids for revenge were common.

Yet on a personal level, Indian culture shuns confrontation. Even the meeting of eyes and the firm handshake were long avoided. Discussions of personal problems were painful. Indians have been known to sit in Government offices for hours before deciding to air a grievance, however just. "My mother won't even get rid of a salesman," says the Navajo's Michael Benson.

For too long, Indian dissent also has been stifled by their forced dependency upon whites for land and livelihood. This has made many of them regard white authority as an almost magical thing. One veteran scholar of Arizona's Hopis, E. D. Newcomer, notes that today's young Hopis even "feel that the god of the whites must be better than their own gods, because the whites have new clothes and shiny cars."

Handicapped by their special definition of dignity and fractionalized by their allegiances to about 300 tribes, the 652,000 Indians in the U.S. have never developed a unity that would sustain massive protest.[1] "Remember, I'm not Indian, I'm

---

1. At the time of Columbus, the native population of what is now the U.S. was probably between 1,000,000 and 3,000,000. By 1860 that had dropped to about 340,000, and by 1910 to an all-time low of 220,000. No longer vanishing, the Indians are now the nation's fastest-growing minority.

RACE 139

Osage," declares Charles Lohah, an Oklahoma judge who finds political intrigue both within and among tribes fascinatingly complex. "Often we have to strap our shields to our backs," he says. But Indians have also watched the nation respond to the marches, sitins and street tactics of restive blacks. Indians feel little affinity with blacks, and there is friction between the races in some federal antipoverty programs; still, the Indians are beginning to demand their share of the action.

That demand is not only just but long overdue. Ford Foundation President McGeorge Bundy insists flatly that "the American Indians are by any measure save cultural heritage the country's most disadvantaged minority." After studying U.S. ill-treatment of the Indian 26 years ago, Swedish Sociologist Gunnar Myrdal described it as "a morality play of profound importance" to American history. He said that it "challenges the most precious assumptions about what this country stands for —cultural pluralism, freedom of conscience and action, and the pursuit of happiness." The morality play is still a bad show today.

The indicators of Indian suffering are appalling. Their life expectancy is 44 years, compared with 71 for white Americans. The average income for each Indian family living on a reservation—and more than half do—is only $1,500. The average years of schooling is 5.5, well behind that of both the black and the Mexican American. Some officials rate 90% of reservation housing as substandard. Unemployment ranges from a low of 20% on the more affluent reservations to 80% on the poorest. The birth rate of Indians is 2½ times that of whites—and a majority of Indians are under 20 years old. The average family has to carry water for its daily needs at least a mile. It is usually done afoot.

Indians, of course, are not statistics, and TIME Correspondent James Willwerth discovered that individual reality for Indians often consists of human deprivation in a setting of uplifting natural beauty. Visiting Arizona's White Mountain Apache reservation, he reported: "The land is like a painting—

hills covered with ponderosa pine, snow-capped mountains in the distance, sprawling valleys filled with thick forests and rushing streams. In the midst of all this, there's a one-room shack with a corrugated metal roof that shows daylight from every angle. This is Judy's house. Judy is in her mid-20s, stocky but not fat, and rather pretty. But she drinks a lot, gets into fights when she does and often ends up in jail.

"Her lovers are legion. The result of one liaison toddles toward me through broken glass and excrement. He's less than two years old. He lived with Judy's sister until recently, but Judy took him back to get some welfare money. Now they are living in this one-room place. 'It's got no windows,' she says. 'But that's nothing. I've never lived in a house with windows.' "

The grim individual vignettes are multiplied among entire tribes. In northern Arizina, religious Hopis fight their uncertain struggle to avoid extinction. Reversing years of decline, the Hopis now number 6,000. Isolated for centuries, even their own villages still have no political links with one another. They live on three massive sandstone mesas in the Painted Desert, where pasture land is scarce and only their skillful dry-farming of corn provides a meager diet.

The sole tribal commerce of the Hopis is a trailer court and a few arts-and-craft shops. Yet the hope of the Hopis lies in their determination to improve their condition. They teach their children to value schooling so highly that the average daily attendance in their elementary schools is a surprising 90% —a rarity among Indians. A score of older youngsters take a bus each day and make a 96-mile round trip to attend high school. Each day 50 adult Hopis get up at 5 a.m. to board a yellow bus and ride 65 miles to their jobs at a BVD underwear plant. Things may get better. Coal has been found on Hopi land, and a strip mine is scheduled to open this year. Ironically, the Hopi devotion to education is diluting what they value most: their own special kind of polytheistic belief that each living thing possesses a human spirit. Now, when elders hold their annual dance with rattlesnakes, many Hopi children laugh.

Agony and Anomie

To live in squalor while surrounded by beauty, to desire a better material life while clinging to traditions is, for American Indians, to know agony and anomie. Their alienation is aggravated by the fact that Indian culture is vastly different from that of the whites in terms of technology, productivity and intellectual interests. From the viewpoint of what makes a modern civilization work, Indian culture appears hopelessly irrelevant. To some extent, the collision of Western and Indian cultures warped the conquerors' attitudes. When the Senecas sought assurances from President Thomas Jefferson in 1802 that their rights would be protected, no attempt was made to bridge the cultural gap. They received a patronizing note from a secretary that said: "Brothers, your father, the President, will at all times be your friend and he will protect you and all his red children from bad people." Only last fall Ted Rushton of New Mexico's Gallup *Independent* wrote haughtily of "the inevitable clash of a superior culture with a vastly interior culture."

The Indian child who attends school with whites must brace himself for taunts: when it rains, he is told, "You must have done your dance." If he has a girl friend, he is asked: "How's your squaw?" Or it may be "Hey, Tonto, where's your horse?" and "What number is your teepee?" "Indian kids are shy, and can't take this," explains Gary Fife, 19, an Oklahoma Cherokee-Creek student at Northwestern State College.

Prejudice is as painful a fact to Indians as it is to blacks. Indians suffer just as harshly from biased history books. One text observes that "it is probably true that all the American Indian tribes in the course of their wandering lived for some generations on the frozen wastes of Alaska. This experience deadened their minds and killed their imagination and initiative." A white teacher in a Chippewa reservation school recently asked Indian children to write essays on "Why we are all happy the Pilgrims landed." Western movies and television, of course, still portray the Indian as the savage marauder. "How are you going to expect the Indian to feel a part of America when every

television program shows him to be a brute or a stupid animal?"
asks Ray Fadden, owner of a Mohawk museum in northern New
York. On an Apache reservation, even an Indian girl was
caught up in the TV drama. As an Indian actor crept up on an
unsuspecting cowboy, the girl involuntarily shouted at the
cowboy: "Get him! Get him!"

Indians smolder when the white operators of trading posts
sell their Indian-crafted goods to tourists at 400% markups.
They resent the white sportsmen who gun down caribou from
airplanes, while their own hunting for lifesaving game is restricted by white laws. They become furious at the white shop-
keepers' use of Indian religious symbols and bad portraits of
Indian chiefs. Don Wilkerson, the Cherokee-Creek director of
the Phoenix Indian Center, claims that a bar in Scottsdale,
Arizona, has a huge picture of a great Indian chief on its roof
as an advertising gimmick. "The Jewish people would not permit such treatment of one of their revered leaders," he says.
"Nor would society allow Martin Luther King to be so humili-
ated."

Alcoholism and Suicide

Dispirited by poverty, rejected by a white culture in which
they are often unable and unwilling to compete, many Indians
choose death or drink. The suicide rate among Indian teen-
agers is three times the national average; on some reservations
it is ten times as high. Shattered by her parents' broken marriage, an 18-year-old Blackfoot girl not long ago killed herself
on her Montana reservation with an overdose of tranquilizers,
though she was an honor student. Accused of drinking during
school hours, a 16-year-old youth on Idaho's Fort Hall Reservation hanged himself in the county jail. Just two days before, he
had talked about conditions on the reservation with Senator
Robert F. Kennedy.

Alcohol has long been a means of escape from boredom and
pressures for Indians. On one Midwest reservation containing
4,600 adults, 44% of all the men and 21½ of the women were
arrested at least once for drunkenness in a span of three years.

Many reservations have opened bars and liquor stores to keep Indians from killing themselves in auto accidents en route home from binges in the city. A much-repeated explanation quotes Bill Pensoneau, president of the National Indian Youth Council, as telling a new commissioner of Indian Affairs: "We drown ourselves in wine and smother ourselves in glue—because the only time we are free is when we're drunk."

The Paternalistic BIA

Sober or drunk, most Indians cite the Bureau of Indian Affairs when they lament their troubles. A unit of the Interior Department, it is supposed to help all native Americans under federal jurisdiction to achieve a better life, mainly by offering education and medical care and protecting their land, water and other treaty rights. More often, it suffocates Indians with its all-encompassing paternalistic authority. An Indian must have BIA permission to sell his land; he is taught by BIA teachers, and if he cannot support his children they may be taken from his home by the BIA and placed in boarding schools or with white foster parents. Most BIA employees are white.

The first Indian head of the BIA in this country was Robert Bennett, appointed by President Johnson in 1966 and admired by most moderate Indian leaders. An Oneida from Wisconsin and a career BIA man, Bennett resigned in dismay last July, charging that "the new Administration has completely ignored the Indians." His successor is Louis Bruce, part Mohawk and part Oglala Sioux, who seems just as frustrated as his people in dealing with the Great White Father. "I keep hearing terrible and sad things that are happening that I didn't know about." One trouble with the bureau, claims one of its most effective field men, is that it is overstaffed at top levels (there is one BIA employee for every 18 reservation Indians), and it takes three years to get new funds to pave a road. "We have created a monster," he says.

Indians have seen countless treaties broken, their lands diminished from 138 million acres in 1887 to 55 million acres today, their water diverted. They are convinced that the Gov-

ernment is determined eventually to dismiss the whole problem by terminating all reservations. Long a favorite white lib-
eral policy, based on the assumption that all minorities will
thrive by being assimilated into the mystical American melting
pot, termination of the reservations is now heatedly rejected
by nearly all Indian leaders. These Indians now want first to
conserve all that is best of their own heritage, summed up in
the slogan INTEGRITY, NOT INTEGRATION. They are thus moving
in tandem with black groups that have rejected integration in
favor of black power. Theoretically, at least, Indians have several advantages over the blacks in moving toward their goals.
They have available a whole federal bureaucracy that professes
to want the same end. While they lack national unity, their tribal
traditions give them a sense of self-identity. And above all,
they have their own lands.[2]

To Keep the Land

To fight to preserve those lands and the water required to
make their acreage livable is a constant one for U.S. Indians.
The Senecas are still bitter about the 10,000 acres taken in 1964
by the Army Corps of Engineers for the Kinzua Dam. The
Senecas were paid $3,000,000, but to them land is no mere mat-
ter of money—it is a spiritual as well as sustaining resource.
The Tuscaroras of New York lost 553 acres to a reservoir in
the late 1950s. They were paid $850,000, only to learn that
nearby Niagara University got $5,000,000 for just 200 acres.
Currently, Indians in New Mexico, Montana and California
are locked in battles with various Government agencies for
control of land and water. The Paiutes of western Nevada have
watched their emerald-green Pyramid Lake, ancient source of
their cutthroat trout, shrink to one-third its former size by

---

2. The first reservation opened in 1853, and the system still includes some
284 BIA-supervised enclaves. Indians are free to leave reservations whenever they wish, but those who do not live on them do not benefit from most
Indian-aid programs. All Indians were granted full citizenship status
in 1924.

various water-diversion projects. The lake's ecological balance has been destroyed, and most of the fish have died.

The most dramatic controversy over native lands is one now raging over the ownership of 90% of the acreage of Alaska. Aided by some of the nation's best lawyers, including former Supreme Court Justice Arthur Goldberg and former Attorney General Ramsey Clark, 55,000 Indians, Eskimos and Aleuts contend that they hold title to the Alaskan land because the U.S. did not purchase it from Russia in 1867; it bought only the right to tax and govern the territory. When Alaska became a state in 1959, the state began to assert claim to the area. It has seized 450,000 acres for itself. The natives are willing to give up all except 40 million acres—10% of the state—at a price of $500 million and a 2% royalty on revenues from the surrendered lands. If they do not get satisfaction this time, the native groups calculate that they have sufficient legal options to tie up the land in court contests for years.

Today activist Indians throughout the U.S. are determined to push all such holding operations to the limit of their resources, since they have seen the devastating impact of closed-down reservations. The Menominees of Wisconsin had good schools and community services, when they were "terminated" in 1961. Since then, many Menominees have had to sell their lands to pay taxes in their new ownership status. The Indian hospital shut down and sawmill profits dwindled. As a result, the state paid out more than six times as much money in welfare to the Menominees as before—and the Menominees lost their identity. "The Menominee tribe is dead," reports Professor Gary Orfield in a study for the University of Chicago, "but for no good reason." Also terminated in 1961, Oregon's Klamath tribe suffered soaring rates in suicides, crime and drunkenness.

There are, however, encouraging signs of progress on some reservations. The Lummi tribe of Washington State, a sea-oriented people along Puget Sound, are using federal funds and considerable hard labor to develop the most advanced aquafarm in the U.S. They control the spawning and cultivating of oysters, the breeding of hybrid steelhead-rainbow trout and the harvesting of algae, used in making toothpaste, ice cream and pudding. It may net $1,000 an acre for the Indians, compared with at most $40 an acre in land farming.

Elsewhere some 150 commercial and industrial enterprises, among them General Dynamics and Fairchild Camera, have moved onto Indian reservations, enticed by the freedom from real estate taxes accorded reservation enterprises—and by cheap labor. They provide jobs and profits for individual Indians as well as their tribes. Simpson Cox, a white Phoenix lawyer, has spent 22 years with the Gila River Pima-Maricopa Indians, successfully pressing the Government to compensate the tribe fairly for confiscating their lands. He has helped them build industrial parks, a tourist center, a trade school, farms, community centers and an airstrip.

Antipoverty funds are also beginning to benefit Indians, since by any definition no group in the U.S. is more impoverished than Indians. One group utilizing such funds is Oklahoma for Indian Opportunity, founded by LaDonna Harris, the attractive, mixed-blood Comanche wife of Senator Fred Harris, chairman of the Democratic National Committee. Her group fights federal red tape to help reservation Indians, gathers evidence when whites discriminate against them, forms buying clubs to combat high grocery prices, trains young Indians for jobs and leadership. There are sharp contrasts in the efforts to help reservation Indians. Navajos at their tribal headquarters in Window Rock, Ariz., have eagerly taken to instruction in the use of a computer to handle industrial-development projects. In northern Minnesota, Indians had strayed so far from their traditions that white sportsmen had to be employed to teach them the rudiments of canoeing, water safety and fishing.

Life in the City

Indians also now have a few influential voices in the U.S. Congress. One of them belongs to Senator Edward Kennedy, whose subcommittee on Indian education recently charged that "our nation's policies and programs for educating American Indians are a national tragedy." Another friend is Minnesota

Senator Walter Mondale. An honorary Chippewa chief, Mondale criticizes Indian schools as containing the elements of disaster. "The first thing an Indian learns is that he is a loser."

The Indians who move off the land and into big cities are indeed apt to become losers. More than 200,000 Indians have done so. They do not congregate as closely as blacks, partly because they meet less resistance in moving into low-income white neighborhoods. There are nearly 60,000 in Los Angeles, perhaps 20,000 in the San Francisco Bay area, about 12,000 in Phoenix, 15,000 on Chicago's North Side. Some 12,000 inhabit the Minneapolis-St. Paul area, almost half in shabby apartment houses and creaky Victorian houses near Minneapolis' Franklin Avenue, which cops and Indians call "the reservation."

TIME Correspondent Richard Saltonstall talked to many Indians who had tried the urban life. "Nobody mistreated me in Dallas," he was told by Donna Flood, a mixed-blood Ponca. "But I was unhappy there. It was too fast. There was noise, fumes, confusion—the white man's problems. In the city you lose your contact and feeling for the land. You become isolated." Hiner Doublehead, a Cherokee with two children, took his family to Chicago. "God, it was a jungle when we got there," he recalled. "The people lived like foreigners—unfriendly, clannish. It was the closeness and the crammed-in living that got to me. The bars were the only places to get acquainted and to unwind. But the friendships never went far. Nobody would invite you up to his house. I didn't feel like I was human up there."

Even the Indians who manage to make it often get restless and long to return to their reservation families for spiritual renewal. Many do so, abruptly abandoning jobs. It is the lure of the land, most often, that proves irresistible. "They used to tell me that the land is like your mother," explains Tom Cook, a 21-year-old Mohawk. "The trees are your brothers, as are the birds in the air and the fish in the water. They give you life; they give you food; they give you everything. It was so pretty the way my grandmother used to tell it." Cook attends college in New York City and is a full-time steelworker in Manhattan.

Something of Value

Indian grievances are specific, but the goals of redress so far remain diffuse. There are no Indian leaders who, with any confidence of national support from their people, can speak on precisely what should be done. Traditionalists merely tend to look at the mountains that have sheltered their tribes for centuries and at the writings of their ancestral prophets, and they say patiently: "We'll outlast you whites." There are others who seek accommodation of white and Indian cultures. Says Ronnie Lupe, tribal chairman of the White Mountain Apaches: "We know what the white man offers us. There are certain comforts in your culture—good homes, good cars, good jobs—but there is a certain way to get these and yet retain our identity, and we have yet to find it."

But even that kind of reasonableness is dismissed by the new Indian militants as the talk of "Uncle Tom-Toms" or "Uncle Tomahawks" and "Stand-Around-the-Fort Indians." What these leaders seem to want most is for the Federal Government, which now spends only $500 million a year on aid to Indians, to increase its spending for Indian schools, roads, housing and medical care—and to stop smothering Indians with restrictive regulations and unwanted advice on how to run their affairs. They want their water and land rights protected and expanded, not contracted through treaty violations. They want help in attracting job-providing industries to their reservations, but they want to determine what kinds and how they will be operated. They want federal benevolence, in short, as compensation for the loss of more than half a continent, but they want to be free to go their own way—even though they are not yet certain of their direction.

The Indians' longing to live harmoniously with nature touches recesses of nostalgia in the minds of many Americans. Indeed, at a time when the drive to protect and restore the nation's physical environment is the most popular cause of the day, whites' guilt over their spoilage of air, land and water engenders a new admiration for those who have fought for so long to protect their own plains, lakes and hunting grounds. It would be wrong to romanticize Indian culture, but there is something to be valued, or at least envied, in a society that respects the wisdom of elders, enjoys the closeness of kinship, prefers tranquility to competition, and sees little merit in 9–to–5 punctuality at a desk.

Although they now live in what one Indian calls "a schizoid world of fractured loyalties," all Indian leaders agree that the best of their ancient heritage is a priceless resource. To many white Americans, who are constantly told these days how much they have to feel guilty about, the demands of yet one more minority may seem almost more than the conscience can bear. Yet Indians can hardly be expected to keep their peace just because they have only lately joined the queue of those vociferously demanding social justice. If they continue to be rejected, many young Indians will continue to despair and will embrace the sentiments of Phil George, a young Nez Perce, who wrote:

> This summer I shall
> Return to our Longhouse,
> Hide beneath a feathered hat,
> And becomes an Old Man.

The new militants reject such resignation, and are determined that Indians be heard along with all of America's second-class citizens. Their aim is nothing less than to reverse the perspectives of the races. Explains one:

> You will forgive me if I tell you that my people were Americans for thousands of years before your people were. The question is not how you can Americanize us but how we can Americanize you. The first thing we want to teach you is that, in the American way of life, each man has respect for his brother's vision. Because each of us respected his brother's dream, we enjoyed freedom here while your people were busy killing and enslaving one another across the water. We have a hard trail ahead of us, but we are not afraid of hard trails.